Poetic Recovery
Life Don't Rhyme
A Memoir

By Zoe Sheppard

© 2009 by Zoe A. Sheppard. All rights reserved.

Published by Miracle Society Book Production and Consulting Company. Brooklyn, NY 11210.

ISBN: 978-0-9791640-9-5

Front cover photographers:

Kevin Sundiata Sheppard
(Zoe Active Addiction)

And

Henry Leutwyler
(Zoe Dress Barn Photo Shoot)
Make up by Bobbi Brown
Suit courtesy of Dress Barn

Back Cover: A Night at the Apollo Theater
Hair by Paula Carnegie

Cover design by Edward Davis III

To my Editorial Team thank you very much for your keen eyes and attention to detail.

Denalerie Johnson, Sarah Carter,
Ciara McFeely, Liz Carey,
Jill Simonson, Erin Moran,
Michelle Puchita, Suzanne Elliott,
Wendy Wilkins, RosalynTaylor O'Neal
and
Esther Barnett

To Sharon Jackson Turner And All The Phenomenal Women We Celebrate

For The Survivors and Volunteers Who Grow
Stronger Through Helping Others

Struggle strengthens the soul. Sacrifice is mandatory. Blessings are the fruit of both.

Acknowledgements

I acknowledge my Lord and Savior who continues to keep me in the midst of it all.

To my Mother who instilled in me the importance of having a God in my life, whose demonstration of faith, a lot of prayer and survival instincts were taught to me daily.

To my Daddy who has always been my hero. Thank you for allowing me to be your princess.

To DuVal Major, you helped me to save my life, as I lay dead in that dark place known as addiction. You asked only four things of me; that I permit you to love me until I was capable of loving myself, and that I become open, honest, and willing.
My love for you knows no end. Thank you Major Dad

To Sue Della Corte, and Gina Shea, Thank you for pushing me to the limit.

To Pamela Spencer, thank you for showing up and showing out on my behalf. You are truly an awesome role model.

TO DRESS FOR SUCCESS WORLDWIDE

To the entire staff and volunteers Thank you.
Shhh I know that you are really angels, but I will keep it our secret

To Joi Gordon CEO of Dress for Success Worldwide. Thank you for my coat. Thank you for showing me, me! Thank you for seeing more in me than what was visible to me in the mirror.

To Walthene Primus for recognizing "Good"
For continuing to be a living, breathing example of professional excellence.
Women of DC 37 Local 957 you rule

**To Every Member of the PWG
(Professional Womens Group)
I thank you for your support**

To Bobbi Brown of Bobbi Brown Cosmetics ,
Thank you for showing me what
you saw all the time. You are Dynamic!!!
To Donna Raiford, you are the angel that God strategically
placed in my life at the right time. You have
promoted my project from day one, and I thank you for
your staunch support
To Vivian Gathers, whose computer proficiency saved the
day. I am deeply in your debt. Thank you
To Lisa Daniell, and the entire staff of Women's
Press Collective of Brooklyn, Thank you

**To the Majoretts of J Gallery
continue to shine**

To my siblings Kevin(Sundiata), Daryl, Robert, Philippe,
Ruther II, Roberta, Alexanderia, Zelda, Marie, and Alicea.
Thanks for the many years you put up with my mess.
Thanks for
opening your hearts to love me when I was content
to stay alone in my mess.
You all have inspired this work.
To my all of my nieces and nephews who never cease to
amaze me. Kevin Jr., Lamonya, Torrrie, Tallia,Pajan, PJ,
Shelby, Faith, Darrell, Brittney, Brandy, Gabriel, Chayse,
Daryl Jr. Bobbie, James and Quincey

To Vernice Warfield, your influence and presence in my life has created a Survivor and a Contender. I will continue to
pray for your soul.
To Uncle Tommy Warfield, remain fabulous and continue to make the world better, with your gift of song.
To Uncle Michael Warfield, you sure know how to throw a party and a wedding.
To Doretha Manning thank you for your compassion.

To Quretta Myles, thank you for loving me no matter what. Our friendships spans four decades and I have enjoyed everyone of them with you. You are a blessing in my life and there is no one like you.

To Adrian Porter, knowing you has been delightful, Thank you, for your many contributions to my life.

To Cynthia (T) Fletcher, thanks for being there and giving a new meaning to the word "Wounded".

To JoAnn Duke, for always keeping it real enough to fall out on the floor and laugh until you know. I got madd love 4 u.
To Ann Valentine, thank you for making sure I never got mugged You are The Diva.

To Lorraine German, know that I love you. You inspire me to go on, and on, and on

To LaMonya Visor and Kevin Sheppard Jr. Thank you for being examples of Young Black Professionals.

To William Edward Young (BaBra), your friendship has never wavered. I will always love you. Thanks for teaching me how to love me when I am alone. You are the finish and the start of Me and I am Loving *You* for My Life

To Beverly (Ninzingah) Sheppard, your spirit and encouragement has taught me just how much love can withstand.
To Betty Barkley, please come back, I love you. To the entire Barkley Family of Rochester, NY thanks for allowing me to be your sister.

To Arlene Rose, thank you for being the most gracious, honest and loving soul I have ever had the pleasure of calling friend
To Judy Murphy I wish you every happiness with *all* your animals.
To Pearice Bundy, thank you for being a soldier in the army.

To Hezekiah Walker, and LFT, Marvin Sapp, Kirk Franklin, Donnie McClurkin, Yolanda Adams, Donald Lawrence and Shirley Ceasar for providing a musical Ministry that inspired this creation.

To my babies, whose accomplishments I celebrate
Jacqueline Farnan, Michelle Williams, Yvonne Scott Ed Coleman, Carla Lyde, Anthony Markum, Roselyn Poyer Linda Ivey, Joann Johnson, Christopher Boston, Helen
Morrison, Leona Jones, Odell Penco, Carrie Booker, Coleen Conenna, Jacqueline Wilks, William Roberts, Cheryl David, Colell Duncan, Toni Luck, Michelle Connor, Linden Shaw, Angel Rodriguez Belinda Shambley, Pauline Sheppard, Candace Budge and Regina Corbett.
(you already know)

Thanks to Women with a Purpose

Ivy Tucker Lucas you are the best teacher and I am a better counselor having known you.

To Errol Sasso, thanks for your patience. You have been my daily source of support and my biggest fan.
I will always love you.

In Memory of Those I Love

To Charlie and Lizzie Sheppard, being your Granddaughter, continues to be a pure delight, I know yall are fussin and fishin.

To Robert Warfield (Daddy Bob), I continue to sing because of your love.

To James Bryant, thank you for finding and loving my Mommy

To Elizabeth Majors Sheppard, who demonstrated the true meaning of devotion. You taught me the art of making a house into a home.

To LaVerne Barkley, being your daughter prepared me for this moment in my life.

To Johnnie Jenkins, for always being my knight in shining armor.

To Wilhemina Myles thank you for opening the door on the 5th floor to your home, when I was ashamed to go anywhere else.

Life Don't Rhyme

Prologue

Shouting, crying, laughing, screaming all these sounds could be heard coming from the hall way of 193 Lenox Avenue aka central booking. They were ignored by the passersby. Hell, this is Harlem and pain and suffering can be heard daily.

It was summer late August I think. The apartment I now occupied was sweltering and there was no breeze coming from any direction. I got the idea that I could cool off if I could jump in the shower, lay still across the futon soaking wet and smoke a crack with the fan pointed in my direction.

The problem was I didn't have any money, no tricks were knocking on the door, and asking for credit for narcotics was a joke. My girlfriend Jackie had been sitting around the apartment with me most the day smoking on and off. She had half dozen babies, and was getting paid for them every month compliments of the State of New York's welfare system. For the most part she gave her mother the majority of the money for the children, since they all lived with her. Jackie always kept some of that welfare money to smoke crack. Since there was good crack being sold in my building it made sense for those who wanted to smoke immediately to come to my apartment. While sitting on the futon Jackie and I discussed where and how we could get some more crack to smoke. I got the bright idea

Poetic Recovery

I could steal the package from the people working in my building if Jackie could locate it. Jackie went down to the first floor to start up a conversation with the pitcher so that she could monitor his moves. He was a young, dumb buck who was a creature of habit. He didn't have sense enough to change up his stash spot. After every customer he served he kept returning the package to his stash under the stairs behind the fuse box. Jackie returned to my third floor apartment and briefed me on where the drugs were hidden. We tried to wait and let some time pass before Jackie would strike up another idle conversation with the worker, so that I could put my plan into action. Crack heads don't have any sense of time. Crack heads are on some "Right Now Time!" We let a mere fifteen minutes pass before I attempted to make my move. Whatever possessed me to think that there was a right way to do wrong?

 Living with an addiction is equivalent to living as a sub-human who is a slave to a drug. Crack was my master an inanimate object whose only job was to bring temporary, euphoric comfort in the form of a cloud to my gravely impaired brain. Being unable to say no to anything that would ensure my next hit only helped to infect my mind, body and spirit with a disease that would ultimately cause me to become estranged from everyone I loved and everyone who loved me. I wished so many times to be able to go back to a

Life Don't Rhyme

time when my life was simple. When nursery rhymes rhymed, when fairy tales were believed and wishes were often thought to have the possibility of coming true.

Poetic Recovery

Zoe Means Life and Life is Not an Audition

Life Don't Rhyme

ONCE UPON A TIME

CHAPTER ONE

The earthquake was loud and more interestingly enough it was in color "red." As my body began to absorb the blows of his fist, I could feel the absence of a tooth. Wham! My head was reeling from the fist that sent my head into a wall. I slumped quickly down to the floor, in an attempt to cover my head from the onslaught of continuing blows. This ass whooping felt as though it was being delivered in slow motion. My brain was repeating the same message over and over. "You know better than to put anyone down with you on a drug robbery you stupid thirsty crack head bitch!"

Quickly everything went dark. The sounds of sirens coming from the ambulance and police cars combined with the walkie talkies startled me out of the fetal position I assumed throughout the assault upon my body. Surprisingly enough when I opened my eyes, which wasn't very wide, I was able to see the EMS workers and police standing over me shouting a barrage of questions at me concerning the identity and whereabouts of my assailant . The extent of my injuries had not been evaluated. I was breathing and for that I immediately thanked God. My vision was blurred and my head felt heavy my lips were swollen and the taste and odor of my own blood confirmed that I was in bad shape. I raised my arms and a sharp pain raced to the top of my

Life Don't Rhyme

head where I placed my hand and found several lumps the size of golf balls. Anyone having survived such an assault would have welcomed medical attention, but not my sick addicted ass! I wanted to find out if the bitch who told on me had saved me a hit.

Yeah folks that's right the same drug that caused my pain was priority. Having satisfied the questions of the police and the examination by the EMS workers I dragged my body to my third floor apartment. To my delight, my snitching ass girlfriend had saved me a hit. She told me that she had no choice but to tell Mike that it was me who had stolen his drugs for fear of receiving a dose of the same pain that had been administered to me. In the shape I was in, I would have forgiven her for anything except not saving me a hit!

Poetic Recovery

Chapter Two

I wasn't always a crack head, to the best of my recollection my life began in Newark, New Jersey. My earliest memories of my childhood began with the sound of my father's voice singing a song entitled "Scarlet Ribbons" a popular love song of the early 1950's.

My daddy sang lullabies to me as a child, and no matter what he was singing I always believed he was singing to me, his princess. Daddy was a handsome 6'3" slender built man. His height, coco colored skin and dreamy brown eyes made him eye candy for any woman who had him in her sights. In addition to his physical attributes, daddy was a charming, intelligent, articulate man with a gift for public speaking. His piercing brown eyes followed your eyes whenever he spoke. My daddy was my own personal Black Elvis Presley. Fine, Fine, Fine!

My mother also sang, though her voice was much softer the melodies were such that I knew she loved me. Mommy stood 5' tall. Her hair was soft, short and curly which enhanced the chiseled features of her beautiful round face. Her eyes told stories when she spoke. Her words captured your heart with her innocence. She literally wore her emotions on her sleeve. When mommy would dress up she became a stunner, to rival Lean Horne and Dorothy Dandridge.

Though my parents were from two entirely different backgrounds, their relationship

Life Don't Rhyme

gave credence to the old cliche` that opposites attract. My parents were barely out of their teens when they married. I can only suspect their need to be loved is what attracted them to one another. They married and from this union I was born Zoe Ann Sheppard and a year later my brother Kenan Bernard was born. The year was 1959 when I noticed that daddy wasn't singing to me as much as he once had. Though I was young I knew something was missing and we now lived in Rochester, New York. In 1960 my suspicions were confirmed. Daddy was no longer coming home to Kenan and I. Something they called divorce prevented him from living with us. That words divorce along with custody and visitation entered my vocabulary crushing my whole world.

THEY CREATED ME

DADDY NEVER CARED IF MOMMY COULD COOK
HE KNEW SHE WAS A WHIZ WHEN IT CAME TO
THE BOOKS
THEN "NANA" GOT INVOLVED AND WOULD
NOT LEAVE THE YOUNG COUPLE ALONE
SHE IS WHAT BROKE UP WHAT COULD HAVE
BEEN A HAPPY HOME
I KNOW THEY LOVED EACH OTHER
AFTER ALL THEY CREATED ME
THAT WAS NOT MUCH CONSOLATION FOR A
LITTLE GIRL WHO'S PARENTS ARE NOW

"DIVORCEES

Life Don't Rhyme

Chapter Three

Nana is a term of endearment. Nana is also what I was instructed to call my maternal grandmother. Nana told to us that she was too young to be a grandmother, and we were to never call her that. It was no secret that Nana disapproved of my Daddy. It is because he was the son of a maid and a sanitation worker that Nana believed herself to be of the upper class. She was a beautiful brown 5' bundle of energy, which I believed caused her to suffer from a Napoleonic complex. She had almond shaped eyes, long black hair which she wore in a bun on top of her head. In addition to a perfect petite figure she too had a gift for public speaking and professed to be an ordained minister. She married into prominence after leaving Texarkana, Texas with my mother. Her in-laws founded one of the first African American Baptist church in Rochester New York. Her husband was a talented musician, veteran and day worker for Kodak. He was not much taller than Nana. He was a solid built man with smooth brown skin and serious eyes. His eyes would light up a room whenever he played the piano or sang. As a child I would often watch as he conducted an orchestra or choir. He was a musical phenomenon we called Daddy Bob. Daddy Bob's entire family had a rich musical background. His brother, Uncle Bill was a famous baritone who studied with the Eastman

Poetic Recovery

School of Music. His wife is a renowned opera singer who is one of the first black women to sing with the Metropolitan Opera. There was no question that Nana had married well. She utilized every moment of her marriage to make sure that anyone who was someone, knew who she was. Daddy Bob was a wonderful grandfather and an equally wonderful father to my mother. He could be counted on to intervene on my mother's behalf when Nana was being a pain in the ass. However, he too tolerated far too much disrespect from his wife. She could often be heard talking down to him. She never missed a chance to inflict verbal and physical pain on my brother and I. Day after day she would take what I can only describe as delight in telling us how ignorant my father's parents were. Hell, she ridiculed and mocked anyone she believed was beneath her including her own daughter. The difference between her and my paternal grandmother was like night and day.

Life Don't Rhyme

LIKE NIGHT AND DAY

ONE GRANDMOTHER COULD NEITHER READ
NOR WRITE.
SHE WOULD TANN MY HIDE WITH A SWITCH,
WHEN I DID SOMETHING BAD OR SAID
SOMETHING THAT WASN'T VERY NICE.
THEN SHE WOULD TAKE ME BY THE HAND
AND LEAD ME INTO THE KITCHEN, TO TEACH
ME TO COOK WHATEVER SHE WAS FIXIN.
SHE TAUGHT ME TO COOK, AND IN BETWEEN
TASTING I WOULD READ TO HER FROM
THE GOOD BOOK.
THERE WERE TIMES SHE WOULD SIT ME IN
HER LAP, AND BRAID MY HAIR.
THAT'S WHEN I WOULD POSE THIS QUESTION
TO HER
"WHY ARE MOMMY AND DADDY NOT TOGETHER?"
SHE WOULD TURN ME AROUND SO THAT I
COULD LOOK DEEP INTO HER EYES, AND WITH
SWEET SNUFF IN HER MOUTH SHE WOULD REPLY
"YOUR OTHER GRANDMOTHER AIN'T FAIR."
THAT IS ALL SHE WOULD SAY AND CONTINUE
BRAIDING MY HAIR.
WHEN THE WEEKEND WAS OVER, DADDY
WOULD TAKE MY BROTHER KENAN AND I BACK TO
WHAT NANA CALLED OUR HOME.
I HATED HAVING TO LEAVE MY OTHER
GRANDMOTHER
GOING TO NANA'S HOUSE, WAS WORSE THAN
THE MOST DREADED DISEASE.
SHE INSISTED WE CALL HER NANA
SHE WANTED US TO BELIEVE SHE WAS A
SERVANT OF GOD.
WHAT I QUICKLY LEARNED, THAT ALL SHE WAS,
WAS A FRAUD.
OH, SHE PREACHED TO A CONGREGATION,
WHILE SHE MADE FOSTER CHILDREN HURT.

Poetic Recovery

SHE COOKED DELICIOUS MEALS,
NOW LET ME TELL YOU THE "DIRT"!
SHE COUNTED WHAT WAS IN HER
REFRIGERATOR, AND KEPT IT LOCKED UP TIGHT.
SHE WOULD KEEP ME IN THE ATTIC IF MY
HOMEWORK WASN'T RIGHT.
SHE TIED ME TO A STEAL BEAM, WAY DOWN IN
HER CELLAR, AND BEAT ME WITH ELECTRIC
CORDS SO NO ONE WOULD HEAR ME YELLIN.
WHEN SHE HEARD ME SAY THE WORD AIN'T
SHE WOULD SAY "AIN'T IS NOT A WORD; YOUR
OTHER GRANDMOTHER USES IT BECAUSE SHE IS
IGNORANT AS DIRT"
THOUGH I WAS A LITTLE GIRL, I KNEW THAT
WHAT SHE SAID WAS NOT NICE.
THE TRUTH IS, LIZZIE SHEPPARD, MY OTHER
GRANDMOTHER LOVED ME MORE THAN ANY
WORDS CAN SAY.
BUT LIZZIE AIN'T HERE ANYMORE. THE LORD
SAW FIT TO LET HER IN THROUGH HIS FRONT DOOR.
I WANT YOU TO KNOW GRANDMA, I LOVE AND
MISS YOU A LOT. IT WAS YOU WHO TAUGHT ME
HOW TO STIR UP LOVE IN A POT

Life Don't Rhyme

Elizabeth Sheppard, better known as Lizzie was a statuesque woman with beautiful golden brown skin, and long black hair. Her round face held the eyes that saw through the souls of the wicked and into the hearts of God's children.
She could always tell whether or not you were a child of God the moment you opened your mouth. She didn't fool around with her grandchildren. She always told you the truth and took a switch to you if you ever lied to her.

    Her husband, Charlie was a strapping 6' 5" hunk of solid black strength. His eyes twinkled and his skin was smooth and black. His hands were large with thumbs that were permanently bent from an accident he survived while working with horses. He worked hard and no matter the task always had a smile, a hug and some peppermints for his grandchildren. With no formal education my grandparents worked harder than any people I know. I am grateful to them for creating my father, an intelligent man who was the first black man to graduate from his high school and went on to become a prominent businessman and a member of the Chamber of Commerce, my father the son of a maid and sanitation worker.

    On the weekend when Kenan and I were visiting our father, we would spend time with my Gramps and Grandma. On Saturdays we would run errands, first stop was the Farmers Market. This is where live poultry and fresh vegetables are sold. Gramps would buy live

Poetic Recovery

chickens and take them home. We would watch in amazement as he chopped the necks off the chickens while their bodies ran around the yard headless. As young kids we found that to be one of the funniest things in the world. Then he would let us help him pluck the feathers off. It was Gramps who introduced my brother and I to stewed chicken feet. This meal was as delicious as it was country. Our next stop was the A&P supermarket. Grandma always made Kenan and I wait in the car. We knew when they came out of the A&P we would each have our own box of animal crackers. We would then go home and put the groceries away only to leave again
for a department store known as Shoppers Fair. Grandma and Gramps bought all of our clothes there for the weekends when we would visit. We never took them back to Nana's house, because we never brought any with us. On Saturday night we all piled into Gramp's Buick and went to the drive-in movie. My childhood took place on the weekends with my Gramps and Grandma. There were times when Kenan and I were left to our own devices. We would pick concord grapes from the fence in the backyard and eat them until we were sick. Once we pretended to be
pirates on a ship in the attic. There appeared to be a hole in the floor of the attic that would serve as a great place to put a sail if we could fit a pole inside it. I found a pole and placed it in the hole. Before I could put my sheet in place to make the sail the pole went straight through the floor to the

Life Don't Rhyme

ceiling below. When my Daddy came home and saw the gaping hole in his ceiling both Kenan and I received the whipping of our lives. I got the worst of it because I was the oldest and should have known better. Kenan and I always fought with each other because I was always bossing him around. One rainy Saturday afternoon we were jumping off the bunk beds playing Superman. Kenan jumped off the top bunk on top of me scratching my face. I became so angry I grabbed him by his neck and rammed his head into the edge of the bottom bunk. This was a bad move because his blood began gushing from his head. Of course I didn't mean to hurt him as badly as I did, which didn't matter because again my daddy tore my ass up. I didn't play Superman again for a long time. Kenan was a great little brother as far as little brothers go. The older I got the more of a nuisance he became. I loved my brother no matter what we went through. Kenan helped me to learn how to ride my bicycle; he let me help him catch wasps and bees in jars. We made tents out of sheets and dug up Nana's garden trying to escape to China. We bathed together in a tub of bubbles made from Tide or Ivory liquid. We walked to and from school together we played Man from U.N.C.L.E and found Ex-Lax thinking it was hidden chocolate only to race to the bathroom all day. We were two children conceived out of love who believed in happily ever after.

Poetic Recovery

Chapter Four

GRAMPS

GRAMPS IS A MAN WHO DOES WHATEVER HE CAN TO KEEP HIS FAMILY HEALTHY AND HAPPY ESPECIALLY HIS GRANDS
HE WORKED FOR THE DEPARTMENT OF SANITATION.
BICYCLES WERE HIS FASCINATION.
HE WOULD PICK UP THE OLD FRAMES HE FOUND WHILE WORKING HIS ROUTE.
WHEN GRAMPS WAS SURE HIS GRANDS WERE ASLEEP, DOWN THE BASEMENT STAIRS HE WOULD QUIETLY CREEP
THERE ALONE HE WOULD TINKER AND BANG AND POUND ON THE FRAMES OF OLD BIKES HE WOULD SAND THEM AND PAINT THEM MAKING SURE ALL SCREWS AND BOLTS WERE TIGHT.
WHEN CHRISTMAS MORNING CAME AND TO MY DELIGHT MY BROTHER KENAN AND I EACH WERE GIVEN SHINY NEW BIKES.

IN LOVING MEMORY OF CHARLIE SHEPPARD

9/13/1906-7/20/2008

Life Don't Rhyme

Now the way I figure it, my parents were perfectly matched. They loved each other however that wasn't good enough for Nana. She went out of her way to cause dissension between my parents. We lived in Nana's house during our early years. She was mean, strict and a professional phony. Kenan and I lived for the weekends. We may not have been able to tell time but on Fridays when the doorbell rang Kenan and I would run out the front door as though we were escaping from Devil's Island. We would jump into Daddy's white Chrysler Imperial relieved we had survived another week in Nana's house. Daddy lived in the same house with Grandma and Gramps on Scio Street. Daddy worked two jobs most weekends. This would leave Kenan and I time to spend with Gramps and Grandma. Most Sundays if we didn't go fishing we would drive out to the country to a town called Williamson, outside of the city of Rochester. This was a rural area where mostly farmers lived. While driving Gramps would put Kenan in his lap so he could pretend to drive. It was tradition when going to the country to stop at our favorite ice cream parlor. They had the best butter pecan and black cherry ice cream I had ever tasted.

My Grandma's sister Earlene still lived on the farm of the family for whom she and her family worked. They were hired to pick crops, cherries, apples, peaches, tomatoes, corn, squash, collard and turnip greens. Aunt Earlene

Poetic Recovery

was given a small patch of land where she and her family lived in a shack with a tin roof. Inside was a pot belly stove that burned wood in the winter. Cherry trees grew in abundance on the property. It was in those trees my brother and I found the perfect treats on warm summer days. Grandma always warned us about eating to many cherries. She said "if you have to shit you will have to use the outhouse." Now, this surely meant, in my mind that there was another bathroom in another house outside of Aunt Earlene's shack. Not! I was given some tissue paper, the kind used to wrap new shoes in when you buy them from the better department stores. I was then pointed in the direction of what was barely a house. What was inside scared the shit right out of me, so I wasn't there for long. I squatted over a giant hole and did my business, wiped and ran like the dickens. I never ate more than a handful of cherries or anything else when visiting Aunt Earlene. During our ride back to the city Gramps and Grandma would have some interesting conversations on Sunday nights. They were centered around the subject of why Mommy and Daddy were no longer married. Nana's name always surfaced as being the one who orchestrated my mother's decision, to leave my daddy. It's too bad kids are not consulted when parents decide to divorce. Kenan and I would have put up some good arguments why it was important to keep our family
together. No sacrifice would have been too

great. Before Gramps or Daddy would drop us off at Nana's house we would remove our new clothes, and replace them with the clothing we left Nana's in. Grandma would always remind us that we were *Sheppard's* and were to always be neat and clean. Hearing these words regularly caused me to become very attentive to my appearance. Through the years I learned that first impressions are made when the first sentence is uttered from your mouth, the manner in which you carry yourself and lastly your appearance.

      My mother always made sure that since I was the only girl we shared quality time together. She allowed me to dress up and wear her high heels. Christmas was always a happy time. Mommy wrapped each gift with pretty ribbons and placed them under the tree she decorated. She bought my first talking doll a Black Chatty Cathy. One Saturday a month she and I would go out to lunch. We would go to the rich section of Rochester on East Avenue. There was a fancy Chinese restaurant where we would sip tea with our pinkies extended and eat with chop sticks. Right next door was an exclusive little girl's dress shop. I don't know how my mother managed to buy me two dresses from that store, but she did. The sacrifices my mother made for me, my brothers and sisters are true demonstrations of unconditional love. My mommy was born to be a mommy and for her presence in my life I am truly grateful.

Poetic Recovery

Chapter Five

As I grew older I began to realize that parents and grandparents teach you what they were taught. In most instances the things they learned are what they swear by. Often they don't want to explore change. They become comfortable in believing that what was good enough for them is also good enough for their offspring.

I was six years old and Kenan was five when we moved into a grey apartment building located at 333 Plymouth Avenue South. I attended P.S.3. It was right around the corner from our new apartment. Often mommy would let my brother and I play in front of the building, because she was able to watch us from the living room window. One afternoon I decided that Kenan and I should go to the playground in the school yard. I didn't think that just because school wasn't in session the playground would be closed, but it was. When Kenan and I arrived there was a chain on the gate making it impossible to get in, well almost. I focused on an opening between the fence and the school building. I told my brother if he could squeeze through he could play on the swings and slide. Kenan slipped through with no problem. When my turn came to squeeze through my head became trapped. Though my body was skinny, my head took on measurements of its own. I was stuck between the fence and the school building. I twisted and turned and could not

Life Don't Rhyme

budge my head. I knew my only savior would be my mother. With tears streaming down my face I screamed to Kenan to go get mommy. When she arrived she was laughing hysterically at what I can only surmise to be a funny sight, me! The sound of a siren from the fire truck followed right behind my mother. Two firemen lifted a
ladder from the red truck and walked over to where I was wedged between the fence and the school building. One fireman asked "are you trying to get into the playground?" I looked at him quizzically as though he had asked the most stupid question I had ever been asked in my six years on earth. Knowing what my future held I answered him politely and said "yes." One fireman lifted me up over his shoulders, while the other brought the ladder around in front of me,
enabling me to place my feet on the ladder. I was lifted high above the fence and slowly lowered to the ground. I was free. I ran straight into the arms of my mommy who was still laughing. Kenan took this opportunity to call me stupid and smarty pants, though I could have done without hearing it. My mother and I thanked the firemen and proceeded to walk home. Apparently mommy knew how embarrassed I was and did not give me a spanking. My punishment would be listening to her tell everyone alive about my ordeal. Mommy knew how to make us all feel good no matter what was going on. The one dish she
prepared to make us smile was homemade banana pudding. Kenan and I would wait for the

Poetic Recovery

bowl and the bag with the crumbs from the vanilla wafers. There was always an argument about who would lick the pot (no instant stuff) and who would lick the spoon. In the end mommy would give us each an equal portion of both putting an end to the bickering.

There were times during those special weekends when Gramps and Grandma had to work that my daddy would take over. He would braid my hair and cook breakfast. Kenan and I both liked to watch him shave with that stinky *Magic Shave*. Daddy would let us help him take it off with a butter knife. He would make sure we were dressed nice and neat. When Daddy was in charge I knew we were going to visit the nice ladies. I told Kenan they were always nice to us because they loved my Daddy. They bought us clothes, toys and let us watch whatever we wanted on the television. I was secure in knowing that I was my Daddy's princess, I also knew that my Daddy was "hot!" I adored my daddy and I thought it was only fitting that these nice ladies should also adore his children. We were a package deal. In today's world one might describe my Daddy as a womanizer. The word wasn't even around back then. I thought as a child that women were just drawn to him because he was handsome. I learned early that relationships are often born from ulterior motives, be they physical attraction or financial gain. Everybody wants something. My Daddy was no different. His goal was to become an

Life Don't Rhyme

independent, successful business man. However, he would require some help in order to see his dream become a reality. Though many women wanted to help him the cost was far too high and he is a proud man. It would be his main woman that would give him the help he needed his mother, my Grandma!

DADDY'S LITTLE GIRL

MEMORIES OF BEING DADDY'S LITTLE GIRL,
ARE THE BESTEST MEMORIES IN THE
WHOLE WIDE WORLD.
NOT A DAY GOES BY THAT I DON'T
REFLECT ON THE PRECIOUS MEMORIES I
WILL NEVER FORGET.
YES, THERE ARE MANY BUT FOR NOW I'LL
SHARE JUST ONE.
IT BEGAN LATE ONE SUNDAY AFTERNOON
WHILE PLAYING WITH MY PAPER DOLLS,
ALONE IN MY ROOM.
TALL, DARK, AND HANDSOME, DADDY
WALKED THROUGH THE DOOR QUICKLY
SCOOPING ME UP OFF THE BEDROOM
FLOOR.
PLACING ME ON HIS SHOULDERS HE SAID
AS WE WALKED OUT THE DOOR,
 "COME ON PRINCESS LET'S TAKE A RIDE
IT'S BECAUSE YOU ARE A GOOD GIRL YOU
CAN HELP DADDY DRIVE."
AS WE DROVE I HEARD THE SOUND OF
MUSIC COMING FROM WHAT SOUNDED
LIKE A MERRY- GO- ROUND THE AIR
SMELLED OF POPCORN,
DADDY SLOWED THE CAR DOWN
HE HONKED HIS HORN, AND PULLED THE
CAR OVER TO THE SIDE
HE SAID "LET'S TAKE A WALK THESE FOLKS
DON'T KNOW HOW TO DRIVE!"
I JUMPED OUT THE CAR AND HE PLACED

Life Don't Rhyme

ME ON HIS SHOULDERS.
STRANGE HOW CLEAR THE MEMORIES ARE
THOUGH I'VE GOTTEN OLDER.
MY EYES OPENED WIDE TO SEE WHAT LAY
AHEAD.
WHAT I SAW WAS A GIANT AMUSEMENT
PARK. IT WAS "SEA BREEZE!"
IT WAS ENORMOUS, STUPENDOUS,
DYNAMIC GIGANTIC, AND IT WAS OPEN
JUST FOR ME.
DADDY AND I PLAYED WELL AFTER DARK
WE SAW FUNNY CLOWNS, ATE COTTON
CANDY, AND RODE THE MERRY-GO-ROUND.
WE RODE THE FERRIS WHEEL, THE
BUMPING CARS AND THE BESTEST RIDE OF
ALL WAS THE JACK RABBIT, DADDY RODE
ON IT WITH ME TWICE.
AND IF YOU WERE TO ASK ME WHAT WAS
MY FAVORITE RIDE I WOULD REPLY;
"EVERY RIDE WE RODE TOGETHER"
DAYS SUCH AS THIS CAUSE MEMORIES OF
ME AND MY DADDY TO LAST FOREVER

Poetic Recovery

Chapter Six

There was one lady who captured my daddy's heart. She also captured the hearts of me and my brother. Her name was Liz, short for Elizabeth. The fact that she shared the same first name as my Grandma was a good sign. The love and understanding she showered us in throughout our lives would definitely cause her to be nominated for sainthood in my book. She was a tall French vanilla skinned black woman, with red hair, freckles and hazel eyes. She was a soft spoken woman, who was undeniably deeply in love with my daddy. I could tell by the way she waited on him as though he were the king of their own private kingdom. It came as no surprise to me when they married during the winter of 1968.

Gramps and Grandma moved from the small house on Scio Street into a two family house located at 857 Jefferson Avenue. Daddy and Liz would occupy the second floor and Gramps and Grandma would take the first floor. Daddy's house had three bedrooms, one for me, one for Kenan and one for daddy and Liz. Our weekends were filled with fresh baked cookies, brownies and of course daily meals served at the kitchen table where we sat down to eat as a family. It wasn't "Leave it to Beaver" or "Father Knows Best" but it was my family and I loved just being a part of something good. I gained two brothers from this union, JR who was

Life Don't Rhyme

my father's name sake and Philippe.
Both boys were handsome, tall, headstrong replicas of my father during their youth. I also learned during this time that I had a sister, Zelda. I had been the only girl up to that point. I was happy to learn that I had a sister who looked just like me and my Daddy. Daddy made a point of making sure all of his children knew each other. I liked visiting Zelda's house. She
had a very nice mother who insisted we call her Ma, or Ruby. She was always kind to my brother and me. My sister Zelda was cute and tall like me and Daddy. She had long brown hair, serious brown eyes and mocha colored skin. She let me play with her toys and ride her bike when I visited. It was cool because we didn't have to share our clothes. Needless to say I always made sure that everyone knew I was the oldest and my Daddy's first born. I loved my siblings and we all shared a common love, our father.

Chapter Seven

Eventually Daddy Bob was blessed after having convinced Nana to adopt two boys of their own. He gave those boys his name and loved them with all of his heart. My uncles Tyson and Mikel were the only children adopted by Nana and Daddy Bob. Furthermore they were the only children to come out of that household unscathed I think. This same household demanded that we attend church every Sunday we were not visiting my father. Now don't misunderstand, I loved going to church, especially with my mother. She didn't attend the same church as Nana. We went to Aenon Baptist church on Oregon Street. It was a small church with a choir and Sunday School. Mommy sang in the choir and participated in any activity that would uplift her spirit. We really got to hear mommy sing in church. Her voice was beautiful when she was singing to Jesus and it made me feel proud to see her marching down the aisle singing "'We're Marching to Zion." The best part of all was watching people get the Holy Ghost. Me and Kenan would crack up after we stopped being scared. We use to play a game in church and pick who the Holy Ghost would get next. In Nana's church no one ever got the Holy Ghost so I just figured maybe the people were afraid to let him in. I learned that God reveals himself differently to different people. It is up to the individual to accept him.

Life Don't Rhyme

Nana forced me to wake up at six o'clock each and every morning to practice the piano. I loved the piano and I loved to sing. Daddy Bob was the one person I could count on to keep me focused on my lessons. He encouraged me to practice, unlike Nana who demanded it. His knowledge of music inspired me. He was gentle when instructing me on how I should hold my hands over the keys of the piano. He sang the scales with me, made sure my posture was straight, and that I always sang from my diaphragm. I took lessons continually for three years. It was the constant drilling from Nana that won out over my desire to pursue the piano. Nana always made me feel inadequate as if I would be struck by lightning if I didn't become the next child prodigy. I was a child who enjoyed music, and singing and she did everything she could to steal my joy. However I performed in my first piano recital where I played a piece entitled Drifting. I wore one of the dresses my mother purchased from the dress shop on East Avenue. I memorized the music and played it as beautifully as I looked. Both Mommy and Daddy came to see me, their princess. I often imagine how painful it was for my mother growing up as a child. I also wonder if it was her childhood and upbringing that caused her to search out love to the extremes she did. Daddy Bob was my mother's only father and she could always rely on him to ease the pain she endured at the hand of her own mother.

Poetic Recovery

Daddy Bob always showed me love,
despite his wife's vicious verbal attacks
surrounding my inability to comply with her piano
practice schedule.
      It was the music that Daddy Bob
provided that made life tolerable. He would play
the piano and teach us songs. Some were from
the hymnal and others were show tunes from
movies and plays such as Showboat, Porgy and
Bess, The King and I, The Sound of Music, Mary
Poppins and my favorite West Side Story. My
brothers and I would pretend we were actors and
perform scenes for anyone who would listen. Little did I know back then, that my ability to act
would save my life more times than I care to remember. Survival skills were instilled in me very
early. I knew in my heart that my life was worth
living. I also realized I would be
challenged daily with situations that required my
faith and trust in God.

IF YOU CAN SPEAK, YOU CAN SING

DADDY BOB WAS A WONDERFUL GRANDFATHER.
HE INTRODUCED HIS GRANDCHILDREN TO CULTURE THROUGH SONG.
HE TAUGHT ME PIANO, AND I MEMORIZED THE SCALES.
HE SAID "IF YOU CAN SPEAK, YOU CAN SING"
THEN MY VOICE SET SAIL
NO MATTER WHAT IT WAS I WANTED TO DO
HE SAID "PRACTICE WILL MAKE IT COME TRUE."
HE TOOK US CHRISTMAS CAROLING AND TO CHURCH.
EVERYDAY HE WOULD BRING HOME SWEETS FROM WORK.
HE TOOK US TO THE RECORDING OF "HANDEL'S MESSIAH."
WE WATCHED AS HE CONDUCTED THE MORMON TABERNACLE CHOIR.
DADDY BOB,
YOU ARE GREATLY MISSED BY A LITTLE GIRL YOU USED TO HUG AND KISS.

9/22/1922 - 1/10/2000

Chapter Eight

Mommy confirmed my suspicions that I was destined to play with boys forever, when she gave birth to a Christmas baby boy, Darien. Darien was a cute baby and he took the place of my dolls for a long time just as Kenan had. What was important to me was that I still got to boss them around. Mommy was working two jobs most of the time and it was my responsibility to look after my brothers, especially once we returned to living in Nana's house. Her house was more of a museum than a home for children to grow up in. We weren't allowed to touch much of anything unless we were cleaning it. We had to wear slippers all the time because the color of her carpet was ivory. One of my chores was to get down on my hands and knees and clean areas of the carpet that were soiled. Kenan was also given nasty chores at a young age such as scrubbing tiny little pink tiles in the bathrooms with a toothbrush. It occurred to me that my mother was taking a lot of shit from Nana during the time Darien was born, because mommy had not been married to his father. The things Nana would say to her own daughter would make me cringe. I cried often. I wondered why Mommy continued to allow her to speak to her in the cruel way she did. It was Nana who taught me what the word bastard meant, because when it was time for her to remind my mother that she was supporting her grandchildren in her house, she took that opportunity and many others to crush my mother's spirit and self esteem into the ground. She would refer to her own grandson as a bastard. Overhearing the conversations caused me to question whether or not Nana was really my mother's mother. I compared her to the animals in the National Geographic magazine who ate their young. Often while daydreaming I would put myself into the storyline of the Shirlely Temple movie "The Little Princess". For those who are not familiar with the story it is about a young girl who was placed in a fancy boarding school for girls, while her father went off to war. When the money stopped coming for her studies, room and board the head mistress kept her on as a student and a servant. She lived in the attic with the other help. She became a charity case and a maid to those students who were once her classmates. In the end Shirley Temple never gave up hope that her father was still alive and would return for her. She soon learned that he had been wounded and was suffering from amnesia. They were reunited with a little help from the Queen of England. Though the lives of my parents had gone through major changes, I never gave up hope that my family would be re-united and we would all live happily ever after. In Nana's house I was the little princess and I suspect my mother was too. I learned that my Father, God will never leave me nor forsake me. My relationship with him will be tested and in my heart I wanted to pass his test.

Poetic Recovery

Chapter Nine

In the years to follow Nana would take into her house countless foster children. For the most part they were treated as badly as she treated her own flesh and blood. Many of those children were without family members. However we all endured brutal punishment. Dinner time was the most dreaded time of day. During the school week Nana would utilize this time to drill all the children who were present at the dinner table on history, spelling, math and of course the Bible. One evening she was drilling Kenan on his multiplication tables, he missed one. There we were at the table trying to eat dinner while being screamed at by our grandmother this Napoleonic, female Hitler. Suddenly she reached across the table with those long red talons that served as fingernails and scratched my brother across his neck. Then just as calmly, as you please she called him an ignoramus; while continuing to drill him some more as the blood ran down his neck. I hated her for hurting my brother. What type of person says they love a child in one breath and maims them in the next? There was also an infant, Donald who had been entrusted in her care. He was a cute bundle of caramel with grey eyes and blond curly hair. He was safe as an infant, once he became a toddler all bets were off. When she decided he should be potty trained that was when my concern for his safety increased. One morning while Nana

Life Don't Rhyme

was checking on Donald in his crib, she discovered he had wet the bed. She became infuriated to the point she hit him so hard she left her finger prints on his little legs. Hearing the screams of this baby I ran into the bedroom to see what was happening. It was then, she instructed me to bring her the hot sauce, a string and some gauze. Fearful I too would feel her wrath I did as I was told and returned with the items. She took Donald's diaper off exposing his penis. She wrapped it in gauze and tied the string around it. She then poured the hot sauce on it. She repeatedly pulled and tugged at the string while Donald cried. She screamed telling him she was going to cut his penis off if he didn't stop wetting the bed. I was in shock that anyone could be so cruel to a baby. It is my belief that Donald must have had an angel watching over him because shortly after that incident a lady who looked like him came and took him away. I never thought about hurting another human being the way I wanted to hurt Nana. To think she actually believed she was teaching this poor innocent child a lesson in bed wetting is unbelievable. Yet she was my grandmother. It was then that I began to pray that mommy would come up with a plan to get us out of this insane woman's house. In anger I would burn holes in her clothes with the iron. There was a time when she was so mean to me and my brother I shaved her mink stole with some hair clippers.
My feelings of dislike heightened to feelings of

hatred every time she would inflict needless pain on any child in that house. I made it a common practice to do and say things I knew she would frown upon. She, with her phony performances in front of her in-laws, her congregation and the social workers who came from the Hillside Children's Center to approve her home for the placement of more innocent children.

    I can't help but wonder what the requirements were in the 1960's that allowed people such as Nana to take in Foster Children into her home. I can testify that whatever the criteria was, it just wasn't thorough enough.

WHAT TYPE

WHAT TYPE OF DAD TELLS HIS CHILD TOUCHING ISN'T BAD?

WHAT TYPE OF MOTHER KEEPS ABUSE UNDERCOVER?

WHAT TYPE OF CHILD SHOOTS HIS CLASSMATE WITH A SMILE?

WHAT TYPE OF TEACHER FONDLES STUDENTS IN THE BLEACHERS?

WHAT TYPE OF PARENTAL CONCERN NEGLECTS A CHILD'S ABILITY TO LEARN?

WHAT TYPE OF QUALITY OF LIFE CAUSES A PRESIDENT TO CHEAT ON HIS WIFE?

Poetic Recovery

AN URBAN NURSERY RHYME

ONE, TWO, BUCKLE MY SHOE

GET OUT OF MY FACE BEFORE I HURT YOU

THREE, FOUR, SHUT THE DOOR

PLEASE, PLEASE DON'T HIT ME ANYMORE

FIVE, SIX, PICK UP STICKS

YOU'RE A STUPID MORON
WHO MAKES ME SICK

SEVEN, EIGHT, LAY THEM STRAIGHT,

ALWAYS SCREAMIN AT ME ITS YOU I HATE
NINE, TEN,

    BEGIN AGAIN
        BEGIN AGAIN
            BEGIN AGAIN

Life Don't Rhyme

    Church became the source of comfort, it allowed me to rid myself of the hatred I acquired while living with Nana through the week. I refused to believe that my God would allow little children to suffer. However maintaining my belief became increasingly difficult. Somehow I managed to hold on to my faith. Because just like the song says Jesus Will Fix It, I knew that some day he would. My biggest questions were; what was taking him so long and would I still be alive when the rescue took place? Unshakable faith is a difficult task for a child, so I held on tight to hope and prayer.

Poetic Recovery

Chapter Ten

During the early 1960's somewhere between James Brown's "Say it Loud I'm Black and I'm Proud" and "We Shall Overcome", my mother met and married a White Irish West Point Graduate. He stood 6' even, with piercing blue eyes, a round red face, and brown hair that receded from his forehead.

His occupation was a tool and die maker. He had a sick sense of humor and an alarming way of keeping my mother in a submissive state of mind. At the time of this marriage, my mother was pregnant with my Thanksgiving baby brother who was the son of an African diplomat who was killed in an airplane crash. It was my understanding that my future stepfather was made aware of my mother's condition before the nuptials. He claimed to love my mother and wanted to marry her just the same. Nana turned out to be (if you can believe it) an ordained minister. Yet her behavior led me to believe she was self proclaimed. Yeah, you guessed it, Nana married them in her home on what was the darkest day of my life and would consequentially also be one of the most memorable days of my mother's life. During this wedding, my brother Kenan and I were present. It was my brother who spoke up first and asked "Why is my mother marrying this White man?" Kenan, though a year younger than I, was smart enough to sense this union had not been blessed by God. As for me, when Nana asked "Is there anyone who can show just cause why this man and woman should not be joined in Holy Matrimony let them speak now or forever hold their peace?" I responded "I can." This answer was quickly followed by a sharp slap across my face by the minister.

  My mother and I quickly learned that what she had married into was another form of hell better known as "domestic violence". Her husband Bob Blake was an absolute alcoholic, who was verbally and physically abusive toward her, my brothers and me. The devil was alive and well and living in our house. An apartment complex known as Chatham Gardens was our new address where we would now live under the pretense of a family. Living there allowed me to experience first hand how other people could be so hurtful toward children with the words that came from their mouths. The ridicule, teasing and questions as to why my mother married a White man were never ending. It caused my brothers and I a lot of grief going to school or to the corner store. Though I can't say first hand that what my siblings endured was as traumatic in their lives as it was in mine, it has certainly raised many questions for which I was unable to find answers for many years. Somehow the phrase "let go and let God" doesn't seem to always work when you are in search of your truth. With all that was going on in my life, I still chose to believe in a God who was a Savior.

Poetic Recovery

I took to watching television on Sunday with my Grandma when Kenan and I visited my Daddy on the weekends. Many of these Preachers raised numerous questions for a young child. One thing I was sure of was that the God I needed had to be great if I were to survive. Through the years I have learned that survival is not enough. Insects and animals survive. As a human being I wanted to live and be happy. Somehow what I wanted did not appear to be within my reach; so I reached for things and people I believed could provide temporary comfort so as to cushion the blows that life would throw my way.

Life Don't Rhyme

Be Healed

Looking for a fairy tale early in the morning.
There he was big as day.
He came without a warning.
For a brief moment I thought I heard angels sing
To my dismay, it was just another
Person claiming to be sent by God lying
The stage was set
Wheelchairs lined up in a row
Each occupant stood up, one by one
The Spotlight strategically positioned
to give them all a glow.
As he touched each person with the palm of his hand
He said the words, "Be Healed"
It occurred to me this person is just a man
How can he heal the sick and the crippled
With just the touch of his hand?
Suddenly reality slapped me in the face, reminding me,
One can only be healed by God's Mercy and Grace
So the next time you are watching television
And a man says "Be healed"
Realize it is not with God,
But the "Sponsors" with whom he struck a deal.

Poetic Recovery

Chapter Eleven

The summer after Mommy married Bob Blake Nana decided my mother and her new husband should spend some time alone. So she took my brothers Kenan, Darien and I on a cross country road trip. The first stop was Texarkana Texas. There we would visit Nana's mother, our great grandmother, Grandma Smith. Our final destination would be Los Angeles California Disneyland. Nana had a brother who lived in Los Angles. We would be staying in his home in a section known as South Central. Nana and Daddy Bob took turns driving and Nana screamed at Daddy Bob the entire trip. I felt sorry for him, because she was so nasty and disrespectful toward him with the vicious things she would say. Kenan and I played a game called "beaver" where we would pick out the station wagons on the highway that had hardwood siding. Who ever called out the most was the winner for the day. We stopped in various motels along the way and saw the beauty of this country in all its glory. The colors were magnificent shades of red, orange, yellow, green and blue. The Grand Canyon and Yellowstone National Park were my favorite sites. I wondered with so much beauty in the world, why were people filled with so much ugliness and hate. I came face to face with prejudice in Texarkana Texas when we were being taken to the movies. At the ticket window a

Life Don't Rhyme

big sign was posted reading "No Niggers Allowed on the First Floor." We were then directed to the balcony. I was angry and shocked. My mother had been taking my brothers and I to the movies in Rochester, New York for as long as I could remember to see cartoon shows on Saturday. Never did we have to sit in the balcony unless it was our choice. That was when I learned and began to acknowledge the Black struggle in America as well as the Civil Rights Movement. That afternoon it suddenly became real and because I was black, I wanted to become involved. I had no idea that Nana, with all her many faults, was an active member of the NAACP (National Association for the Advancement of Colored People). It would be Nana who would bring the struggle right into her living room. It was Nana who would make the historical trip to Washington D.C. to hear Martin Luther King deliver his speech "I Have A Dream." Yet this woman lacked human compassion for her own family. How could this be?

    Nana's mother, Grandma Smith lived in a small wooden yellow house with an indoor toilet which scored big points with me. I and my brothers slept on the floor of an enclosed screened porch. It was equipped with squeaky wooden floor boards which served as a good source of scary late night fun. We made a tent and took a flashlight to bed. The night air was clean, the sky clear with multitudes of stars

Poetic Recovery

which made up the Constellations.
The sounds of small animals and crickets contributed to our giggles and screams throughout the night. During the day I paid close attention to the adults. I soon saw the similarities between Nana and her mother. Though Grandma Smith was a much gentler woman than her daughter, she still had that authoritative presence and verbal harshness that told you she was not to be challenged. Grandma Smith cooked gigantic meals for breakfast and dinner. I figured out it was she who taught Nana how to cook. So it bothered me that Nana had not taught her own daughter. Now Nana's father, Grandpa Smith was a quiet presence in his own home. He took care of a beautiful garden where they grew their own vegetables. I immediately identified the similarities between Nana's husband Daddy Bob and her father Grandpa Smith. The women these decent men had chosen for wives left me wondering if they had both suffered some sort of brain injury early in life that went unnoticed. What I would soon learn was that relationships feed off of, or nourish the participants. My Daddy Bob was led to believe in order for him to achieve his greatness he would require the cold strength that only Nana possessed.

    The highlight of the trip to Grandma Smith's house was the discovery of "slingshots". Across the street from her house was an old unoccupied dilapidated wooden house with

Life Don't Rhyme

windows that were partially broken. My brothers and I took aim daily when there was nothing planned to do with our aunts and cousins whom we had recently met. We had a good ole time competing with each other's distance. When it was time to depart from Grandma Smith's house, we were instructed by Ms. Nana kill joy herself to leave our slingshots behind. Fat chance! We kept them hidden and out of sight until we were given another opportunity to demonstrate our newest skill as slingshot experts. I had been told that Nana had twelve siblings, so I didn't find it at all strange that during our visit the few that still lived in Texarkana had no great desire to be in her company. She obviously was as mean a sister as she was a grandmother. I learned that baggage can be carried into generations if you carry it. I can only imagine that Nana carried trunks, and heaved them on top of anyone she thought would open them and expose their contents.

Poetic Recovery

Chapter Twelve

Upon our arrival in Los Angeles we drove up in front of a sprawling split-level ranch style brick home on a tree-lined street. Nana honked the horn and a tall handsome man with processed black shiny hair, deep brown eyes and smooth mahogany colored skin came out to the driveway to greet us. He had beautiful white teeth and a presence that immediately let you know he was running things and in control. He instructed us to call him Uncle Arthur. I took to him immediately because he reminded me very much of my father. Nana's brother was a funeral director and mortician. There was nothing morbid or lifeless about this man. He drank, danced, preached and loved women. I reveled in the fact that he did not pay any attention to his sister and had no problem telling her in no uncertain terms that she was going to be nice while she was under his roof.

The next day we all prepared to go to Disneyland. We got up early, bathed, ironed our clothes and primped in the mirror. Uncle Arthur had a funeral to oversee that morning and said he would be unable to join us. I had an outfit picked out that I wanted to wear and Nana told me to take it off and put on something else or I would not be going anywhere with her. I muttered under my breath "Bitch, you make me sick!" She claimed to have heard me and said that I would not be going anywhere with her and

Life Don't Rhyme

certainly not to Disneyland. She said my mouth was filthy. I called her a bunch of bitches after that. I had endured the long drive to Texarkana and sleeping on the floor and she had the nerve not to take me to Disneyland. I was livid! She left me and ordered me to stay in the house. I was alone all morning watching television in Uncle Arthur's room. It wasn't until 2pm that afternoon that Uncle Arthur came home from the funeral and found me watching television in his room. I told him what happened. He said, "she is my sister and she has always been a bitch with good hearing!"

      What he said and did next made me feel so special. Uncle Arthur told me to get my shoes on. I still had my original outfit on that I intended wearing earlier to Disneyland. After checking my appearance in the big mirror that was in Uncle Arthur's room, he and I deemed me cute enough to hang out with him for the entire day. Uncle Arthur drove a candy apple red convertible Jaguar. As we walked to the car he announced that we were going to Disneyland. I was ecstatic. I screamed with delight as I jumped up and down kissing him on his smooth face. I didn't care about anything else. I was in love with my Uncle Arthur and the fact that he took great pleasure in going against his sister was icing on the cake. We didn't return until close to 2 o'clock in the morning. We went on every ride I wanted to go on. He bought me a candied apple, cotton candy, soda and popcorn.

Poetic Recovery

I saw all my favorite Disney characters, and to top it off, Uncle Arthur made sure I had all the souvenirs I could carry. The next morning at breakfast Nana didn't say a word to me and I said nothing to her. The silence confirmed that I had won that round. The trip back to Rochester was filled with the sounds of Nana ranting and raving about Daddy Bob's driving. I refused to let her steal my joy or the precious memories I had of that summer.

    I was excited about returning to Rochester. I wanted to share the details of my trip with my mother. I would be going to a new school and living in a new house. I had no way of knowing just how drastically my life was about to change. Had I known I am sure I would have begged my Uncle Arthur to let me remain in Los Angeles with him.

Life Don't Rhyme

Chapter Thirteen

When we returned from California we returned to Chatham Gardens with Mommy and her new husband. It was a nice apartment with three bedrooms. One bedroom was for me the other for my brothers who had to share and the third for Mommy and her husband. We attended Saint Bridget's Catholic School off of Clinton Avenue. I was in the fourth grade and came home for lunch. I made friends easily, and befriended two girls who were twins, Tasha and Terri. They had a brother Terrence who had just come home from Vietnam. I went to their house on several occasions after school to study and do homework. He was always there telling me how good I looked. Finally during one of my study dates with the twins he invited me to have lunch with him the next day. I was thoroughly swept off my feet to think an older man would have an interest in me. Not! What I was served was more than lunch. He attacked me at the door. He ripped my white cotton panties with the pink flowers from my body and raped me. No kisses, no hugs just straight up and down brute force. I wasn't concerned about anything except making sure that I was not pregnant. I stopped speaking to the twins because I believed they knew what was going to happen and were just that vicious to set me up. They believed because my stepfather was white that I had everything they didn't. I was bigger than most kids my age

Poetic Recovery

and found out the hard way that I had to choose my friends carefully. As it turned out I actually had nothing in common with the twins. I was always attracted to older people because I was in this great race to become an adult. I didn't have to search far to find new friends. My hair was cut short back then and I had taken to wearing it like Twiggy the model from London. I would frequent a local barbershop on Joseph Avenue called Lou's Barbershop. It was there I would meet and become friends with three teenage girls Velma who was seventeen and her sister Tess who was 19 and also Jo seventeen who lived on the first floor in the same building as Velma and Tess. They all lived in Hanover Housing Projects. They taught me how to wear makeup, smoke weed, what to drink, and what to say to a man to get what I wanted. More importantly I needed to know what to take to make my menstrual cycle appear. Sure enough my girls came to the rescue. The magic pill was called *Humphrey's 11* when combined with a pint of gin, and a hot bath it was the perfect contraceptive of its time. I never told a soul about that rape because somewhere in the back of my young mind I didn't think anyone would believe me. I became cautious about the way I carried myself in the presence of men. I would often sneak out of the house late at night, which was easy because we lived on the first floor. I would go to Velma and Tess's house instead of going to school at least once a week to get schooled on the subjects of men and sex. My girlfriends never questioned me about why my mother married a white man. They were very sympathetic when it came to the ugly racist remarks I received from the general public. They provided me with that sense of belonging that I was in constant search of. It would be my barber who would be my first lover, he was in his late thirties and of course I lied, saying I was much older. He did my hair, gave me money, and taught me how to play numbers and make love. The back of Lou's barbershop served as an afterhours spot on Friday and Saturday nights. Those were my nights to sneak out of the house. Once he discovered whose daughter I was, he began to give me the cold shoulder. I learned that the mention of my father's name caused some people to reconsider their true intentions when dealing with me. I really enjoyed the rush knowing that some men were willing to take a chance. When Thanksgiving arrived so did my brother Brandon. He was a beautiful, healthy black, happy baby with a patch of gray hair in the top of his head. Brandon rarely cried. He had the blackest smoothest skin I had ever seen or felt. He truly resembled the son of an African king. He liked to play in his jolly jumper a device created in the 1960's that could be suspended from the top of any doorway. Brandon would jump until he fell asleep. He didn't require more than a clean diaper, food and milk. I had become the designated baby-sitter and never had time to

Poetic Recovery

myself. I was always babysitting my three brothers. After they stopped being cute I became bored. I only saw kids my age while in school or church. I also became bored with their childish chatter about toys and games. Bob Blake appeared to like Brandon and made sure Mommy had a diaper service and everything Brandon required after all, he did bear the man's name. I soon found out it was all an act.

One summer night when my stepfather was working late I was instructed by my mother to make sure that the kitchen was clean and the floors mopped. I had almost completed the kitchen with the exception of mopping the floors. While in the process of stacking the kitchen chairs against the front door, suddenly a drunken red faced figure reeking of alcohol burst through the door knocking the chairs down screaming "What the hell are you doing, trying to kill me?" He barged past me throwing the remaining chairs out of his way. He began screaming at my mother "why isn't this fucking kitchen clean? And why are these kids still up?" All I could hear was the sound of his voice cursing my mother and the odor of the liquor that trailed behind his every step made me nauseous. What happened next was a series of events that changed my life. My mother screamed at him telling him that the house was clean and all that was left to be completed was the mopping of the kitchen floor. It was then that I heard him smack my mother across the face. My baby brother Brandon was in the room with them both. My mother yelled to me to get the kids out of the house. I took my brothers Kenan and Darien outside. I assumed Mommy would get Brandon since she was already in the room where he was. It wasn't until we were all outside, barefoot, half dressed, crying and scared that I realized Brandon had been left behind.

    The next thing I saw was this White man with a long butcher knife in one hand and my baby brother Brandon under his other arm. He was screaming to my mother "get back in this house bitch before I cut this little nigger's throat." Thankfully by then the neighbors had called the police. As the police officers approached my mother's husband, he dropped Brandon to the ground along with the knife. Brandon didn't cry nor did he have a scratch on him after landing on the ground. Nana arrived and took me, my mother and brothers back to her house. The next morning my mother went to the police station where she refused to press charges. When I was informed that she went home with him the same day, I was mad as hell. I knew that if I was to survive this episode of my life I would have to speed up my growth process and fast!

    Mommy came to pick us all up from Nana's house later that week. Though I was not happy to be back under the same roof with this man, I endured it. It was because of the love that I had for my mother, brothers and another

Poetic Recovery

new addition my mother was carrying that I hung in there. Daily I would pray, that this great God I still believed in would have mercy and strike this monster my mother had married dead. Surely my God wouldn't let little children suffer. For some strange reason, I thought that God had made the Vietnam War first priority over
my prayers because my mother's husband continued to exhibit his alcohol induced tirades to the point that we were asked to leave Chatham Gardens. We then moved to 173 Bartlett Street in a predominately Black neighborhood in Rochester. I felt good about the move because it was less than a ten-minute walk to my father's house. I knew that if I had to, I could escape. I wasn't a psychic, but you didn't have to be a rocket scientist to figure out that a bi-racial couple in a primarily black neighborhood in the 1960's was certainly a recipe for unrest. The chaos erupted on Bartlett Street without warning whenever Bob Blake drank. I witnessed him kill a mouse with a kitchen fork. He then let us know what a warped mind he had when he administered disciplinary action upon my brother and I. Beatings us to the music of Beethoven's 9th symphony with the live cannons or sending us to run around the block in the snow fifty times. Oh, Mommy didn't escape punishment; he would just take an ax and chop up a piece of furniture he knew she liked. *Talk about memories whew!*

Life Don't Rhyme

God Bless The Child That's Got His Own

Poetic Recovery

Chapter Fourteen

There were a few episodes when my father wasn't always welcomed to pick my brother and I up for our court ordered weekend visits. I later learned that once again, Nana had planted a seed in the mind of my mother telling her that frequent visits with our grandparents and father caused us to become hostile toward my stepfather. *Like we weren't justified in our own right!* When we did visit Daddy we told him about our mother's husband. I could see in my father's eyes how helpless he felt. He told us that unless the court gave permission for us to live with him permanently; we would have to be satisfied with weekend visits. He let us know that he could also be placed in jail if we came to his house as a result of running away from home because he was bound by law to report it. I, for one would have rather died than see my daddy locked up. Aside from protecting each other Kenan and I also had to protect my brothers Darien and Brandon.

The next episode that comes to mind is when we as a family were returning from the "Lilac Festival" a yearly event that takes place in Rochester celebrating the beauty of this fragrant flower. It had been a pleasant day seeing all the flowers out in full bloom, filling the air with its magnificent fragrance. My brothers and I were playing in the park enjoying sandwiches and Kool-Aide my mother prepared for the afternoon outing. Mommy was good about making sure we went out together as a family, even when she was a single parent. Not a weekend went by that we didn't go the movies, museums, parks or the beach. This weekend was no different. As the sun began to go behind the clouds inviting dusk to take its place it seemed that another cloud appeared over the head of my mother's husband. He consumed many beers throughout the afternoon. I could smell the beer on his breath when he yelled "Get the fuckin kids together and let's go." A voice in my head gave me a loud warning, telling me to keep my eyes open and to keep myself and my brothers away from what I believed to be impending doom. As we began to exit the park, my stepfather picked up my youngest brother Brandon and placed him on his shoulders as he was just a toddler and unable to keep up with the pace. As my brothers and I walked briskly over what is known as the Plymouth Avenue Bridge which extends over the Genesee River we turned suddenly hearing the sound of my mother's voice screaming "no, don't hurt my baby, please stop!" At that moment time stood completely still as my eyes and the eyes of my brothers widened in fear of what we were witnessing. My stepfather, with his eyes glazed over in a drunken stupor, screamed at my mother "if you ever try to leave me I will kill you and all your fuckin kids." With that being said, he began to dangle my brother Brandon over the guard rail of the bridge by his feet, pulling him

Poetic Recovery

up and down. My mother was hysterical and we were screaming and crying, pleading for this maniac not to kill our brother. So as not to bring unwanted attention to himself, he handed the baby over to my mother. Though I could see the relief in her face, her eyes were still filled with fear. We walked the rest of the way home in silence. April 4th 1968. Martin Luther King Jr. was assassinated and the riots began. We lived in a black neighborhood with a white man and total havoc and chaos was taking place all around us. My oldest brother and I prayed that night for the family of Dr. King as well as our own. We forgot about forgiving people and took this opportunity to beg God to have someone anyone-come into our house and lynch our stepfather. God has a weird sense of humor, because he ignored our request. Many times we asked God to intervene to no avail. I learned later that what we were praying for was wrong. Though this man inflicted torture and fear into our lives it was up to us to have faith and let God handle his business. As time passed my mother's relationship with this man worsened. There were constant arguments, and fights. He destroyed rooms full of furniture and disrespected my mother regularly. I applaud my mother and her ability to endure this torment for the sake of her children. Though the love of a mother exceeds any love in existence, I impatiently waited for the moment when her love of self would take over her emotions and enable her to open the door to escape. It was clear to me that I couldn't and wouldn't wait for this to happen. I began asserting my independence in ways that can only be described as selfish, rebellious and reckless.

    I was a child forced into an evironment that no child should have to endure. I never once stopped loving my mother, and she never stopped being a loving mother. I came to understand it was because she was a mother, she felt she had to endure the torment and abuse she suffered in order to keep her children safe, clothed, sheltered and fed.

    I learned through the years that my mother's demonstration of strength was exhibited daily. It was because I was a child that it just didn't make sense.

Poetic Recovery

JUST BECAUSE

IT WAS TWENTY DEGREES BELOW ZERO OUTSIDE
IN THE SNOW.
THE MAN MY MOTHER MARRIED MADE MY
BROTHER AND I RUN AROUND THE BLOCK,
50 TIMES IN BOOTS WITHOUT SOCKS.
HE SAID IT WAS PUNISHMENT, BECAUSE OUR
CHORES WERE NOT DONE.
I TOLD MY BROTHER "ONE OF THESE DAYS
I WOULD REALLY RUN"
THOUGH BEFORE I COULD, HE CHOPPED THE
ENTIRE HOUSE OF FURNITURE INTO WOOD.
THEN, HIT MY MOM, JUST BECAUSE HE COULD.
DID I MENTION THAT HE BEAT MY BROTHER TO
THE TUNE OF BEETHOVEN'S 9th SYMPHONY
AT AGE ELEVEN THERE WAS NOTHING
I COULD DO,
OTHER THAN TRY TO STAY ALIVE.
THEN A FEW MONTHS LATER MOMMY WENT TO
HAVE A BABY, VERY LATE ONE NIGHT,
BEFORE MY SISTER WAS BORN,
HE RAPED ME JUST BEFORE
THE SUN KISSED THE DAWN.
SO WHEN MOMMY CAME HOME, I TOLD HER
THE TRUTH AND TO MY SURPRISE HER
RESPONSE WAS "YOU'RE A LIAR,"
SUDDENLY MY HEART FILLED WITH FIRE.
A HATRED SO INTENSE, I THOUGHT IT WOULD
NEVER LEAVE.
BUT WHEN MOMMY MARRIED THAT MAN,
SOMETHING JUST DID NOT FEEL RIGHT
I NEVER THOUGHT ABOUT HATING HIM,
JUST BECAUSE HE WAS WHITE

Life Don't Rhyme

I watched this man take an entire house full of furniture and chop it up with an axe and throw it from the balcony because my mother had another epiphany and attempted to leave him again, only to return. It became more personal the night my mother went into the hospital to give birth to her fifth child Rachelle. It was early in the morning that he entered my room. It was a little girl's room. The furniture was baby blue with gold trim. There was night stand with a lamp and a lamp shade made of baby blue and white lace. The four poster bed had a lace canopy over the bed fit for a fairytale princess. There was a rocking chair, stuffed animals and a portable television given to me by my daddy. I had a doll collection spread across the dresser top and the bed. All the eyes of the dolls appeared to have opened wider as he crept closer to my bed. That night the little girl who occupied that room died. He shook me awake, telling me that my mother had gone to the hospital and that I had to be the mother of the house in her absence. He then crawled into my bed, placing his hand over my mouth. What I remember most is the smell of beer on his breath as his hands reached under my nightgown, saying "It's all in fun, relax and don't make a sound or I will kill you and your mother." I wanted desperately to scream out for my Daddy, but could not. The memory I can't rid myself of is how heavy he felt on top of me and the rancid smell of his awful breath, breathing heavily, with each movement. When my mother returned from the hospital, I told her what happened. She said, "You shouldn't make up such stories, all you want, is to break up our family." She called me a liar and sent me to my room. After that day it would be 36 years later before she would acknowledge this event took place and ask for my forgiveness.

My experience with my stepfather did not place me in a frame of mind where I thought all white people were bad. I was often the only black child in many of my classes throughout elementary school. However what it did do was cause me to believe all men were to be used before they could use me!

It baffles me to this day how I as a child I could dismiss this incident in my life just as my mother had done. It was never spoken of again. It did invade my dreams when I was younger; however, I was always rescued. I have since rescued myself from those demons of the past and they no longer hold me hostage.

ALL IN FUN

HE COMES FROM WORK LATE AT NIGHT
SAYS "I'M GOING TO CHECK ON THE KIDS
TO MAKE SURE THEY'RE ALRIGHT".
HE COMES STRAIGHT TO MY BEDROOM
DOOR IGNORING, ALL OTHERS IN SIGHT.
AS HE TOUCHES ME IN PLACES HE SHOULD NOT,
I SHUT MY EYES AND TRY TO SCREAM,
BUT COULD NOT
THOUGH IT WAS OVER AS QUICKLY AS IT HAD BEGUN
MY STEPFATHER KEPT TELLING ME
"IT'S ALL IN FUN"
I TRIED TO TELL THE TRUTH WAY BACK THEN,
NO ONE WANTED TO BELIEVE A CHILD OF TEN.
SO I PRAYED EVERY NIGHT FOR THE STRENGTH TO RUN
SO I WOULDN'T HAVE TO HEAR
"IT'S ALL IN FUN"

Chapter Fifteen

Shortly after that incident I ran away, was found, and sent to live with more white people; my piano teacher Arlene and her husband, Dan. They were the equivalent of Ozzie and Harriet without children. They were a decent newly married couple who offered to intervene because they genuinely believed in my talent and more importantly Arlene had a growing concern for my safety and felt a new environment would be a welcomed change. I was the first to notice that my behavior was changing for the worse.

I had stopped applying myself to my musical studies and school was no longer of interest to me, other than it being another way to get out of my house. I also believed they were trying to clear their conscience of some hurtful thing they may have thought or said in the past that may have been considered racist. So why not take the confused little black girl into their home? They were very good to me at a time in my life when I believed that I didn't deserve anyone to be good to me. It was a time when I was not being good to myself. After all I had been living in what I can only describe as hell! Whatever their reason for bringing me into their lives and their home I was then, and remain grateful to them. They were wonderful people who treated me as a young adult and not a child. That also scored a lot of points with me. I continued to take piano and voice lessons and enjoyed life as a young teenager. Arlene began to teach me how to play the harp. She played many instruments, however the harp was her first love. In addition to piano lessons she also gave me voice lessons. I performed in another piano recital and sang in Italian. Arlene was the music director for the HOCHSTEIN SCHOOL OF MUSIC. There was an advantage to living with someone who is in the loop of the music world, no matter the genre. I enjoyed singing opera as well as attending performances. I have managed to hold tightly to those memories with Dan and Arlene. They truly gave me hope at a time in my life when I felt hopeless. I learned that love has no color. When help is offered all that is needed is, that it be accepted in the same manner in which it is given.

Chapter Sixteen

With all that was going on in my life my daddy opened a jazz club and restaurant called Shep's Paradise on Clarissa Street. For thirty-five years it would serve as one of Rochester's cultural night spots for blues and jazz entertainment. The music was complimented by great food prepared by Lizzie, my grandma. She became famous for her delicious barbeque sauce, collard greens, potato salad, chitterlings and sweet potato pie. Though I was young I took the position of being my grandma's helper during my weekend visits. I met many talented artists such as Smokey Robinson and the Miracles, Arthur Prysock, Chuck Mangione, Esther Satterfield, Philly Joe Jones, Irene Reid and a host of others. Whenever there was a concert of any kind the visiting musicians would flock to Shep's Paradise knowing they would be greeted with a home cooked meal and the sounds of the local talent. Impromptu jam sessions became a regular occurrence.

    Because I was a tall girl I was often mistaken to be much older than I actually was. It was because of my age that I could not serve liquor and was restricted to the dining area of the club. However I never corrected anyone who thought I was older. My daddy knowing that I was not honest about my age, made it his business to inform everyone who might want to talk to me longer than it took to place an order

Life Don't Rhyme

that I was his daughter and only eleven. It was the tone of his voice that let everyone know that I was off limits to any conversations that did not pertain to the menu. In an attempt to turn me into a lady I was given modeling classes at Edward's department store. I modeled regularly for the teen department on Saturdays. Daddy would buy me each outfit I wore in the shows and I loved him for that. Yet, I still sent my daddy through a lot of changes. I understand that it is because he is my daddy that he continued to show me love even when I demonstrated the behavior of a common street walker. This behavior caused him embarrassment. Being Shep's daughter came with a lot of responsibility that I found difficult to live up to. I couldn't find the voice that would allow me to tell my father that I needed him to be my knight in shining armor and save me from the evil wizard who had cast a spell on my mother, leaving me labeled as a liar, alone and defenseless. I was afraid of not being the only princess in his life, this position that was mine alone. More importantly I was afraid if he found out what my stepfather had done he would commit murder; and I didn't want my daddy in jail!

Chapter Sixteen

There came a time when I didn't think I needed to be supervised by anyone. I was staying out past my curfew, and continued to skip school on a regular basis. I was still smoking cigarettes and marijuana and to make matters worse I lied about anything and everything. Eventually I left Dan and Arlene's home, because they were relocating out of state.

It was during this time my mother began to slowly come out of denial realizing that her life and the lives of her children were in danger. With her sixth child on the way she continued to sleep with the enemy. I returned to live with my mother and her deranged husband. He finally decided to buy my mother a house, located at 6 Englert Street. It was during this time that I would meet my best friend and my first love. My best friend Lettie and I hung out together daily after school. Lettie was a beautiful girl with big brown eyes similar to Diana Ross. She was tall and slender with long bright curly red hair. More importantly she was whiz kid in school who received nothing but A's. She told me she had a brother whose name was Ellis. After meeting him I can only describe my feelings as a dangerous infatuation. Ellis was tall dark and handsome with beautiful brown eyes that held my attention. Every time he spoke, he exposed the most beautiful white teeth that formed a perfect smile leaving me breathless. He was 18 and I was eleven years old going on twenty. By this time I was fairly developed enough to lie and say I was 16 and get away with it. Though I had sworn Lettie to secrecy I am sure she told her brother the truth; since she too adored him. After school I would stop by my Daddy's bar and do his bookkeeping. I had access to money and never missed an opportunity to take what I rationalized to be my share of unpaid child support payments. Ellis became my first obsession. I was consumed with him, and did what I believed would hold and keep his interest in me. He was older and paid attention to me. He convinced me that if I was going to be his woman I had to sacrifice and make sure he had the things he needed; namely, expensive Alpaca sweaters from an exclusive men's store. I bought the affection of this man. Oh, I was young, stupid and naive to say the least, but not for long. I soon began to notice that Ellis never wore the sweaters I purchased for him with the money I had stolen from my Daddy. It wasn't until I actually witnessed him hawk up a mass of phlegm from the depth of his lungs and spit right into the face of his baby's mama that I knew not to question him about anything, yet alone some sweaters. I allowed him to continue feeding me the lame excuses he had readily available. Such as telling me they were in the cleaners or he let his brother wear one and it got messed up in a fight. One day I dropped by Ellis's mother's house and found her distraught and crying.

Poetic Recovery

When I questioned her as to what was wrong she told me some money was stolen from her purse, and she believed Ellis had taken it. It was then that I learned he had been returning the sweaters to the store to buy heroin. My knowledge of the dangers of drugs was non-existent. I had no clue as to what using this drug or any drug could lead to. However Ellis would never offer or invite me to use any heroin with him. He said I was too young, and that he didn't want me to get a habit. He also fed this same excuse to me as a reason for not having sex. I took to be a sign that he loved me and was he was protecting me from something that was bad. Whatever his reason I am eternally grateful. I thank God for the way a young mind interprets things. I was hurt about his returning the gifts I bought for him though not enough to entertain the thought of letting him go. His mother warned me to stop seeing him. She said "he is my son, but when he is using dope he becomes someone I don't like and am ashamed of." The hurt in her eyes was not enough to make me leave Ellis alone. He taught me how to forge checks. I learned I had a knack for signing the signatures of other people. He and I went on a rampage forging welfare checks he had stolen out of mailboxes and he never got caught. My father noticed his money was disappearing and had heard about this relationship and immediately stepped in. He began with firing me and went on to inform me that I was a fool, who had better straighten up her act or I wouldn't be his daughter. He threatened to put Ellis in jail for contributing to the delinquency of a minor. Hearing this from the only man I truly loved devastated me back to sanity for a minute. My search for love would lead me to the best and the worse, and back to the best again.

  I found out later that my Daddy and Ellis's father and uncle were acquainted through business dealings and that locking up Ellis was a scare tactic. I did give him up, but only because he violated parole and was returned to Attica State Prison on a parole violation. The violation was for driving his mother's car without a license while on parole. We began to correspond with one another through the mail and I continued to profess my undying love for him. He convinced me to bring heroin to him in prison taped in the bottom of a brown paper bag during a visit with his mother and sister. It was soon after this episode that the content of his letters changed. He began making amends to the people he had harmed during his active addiction. Each letter I received taught me that life was not a game to be played haphazardly. He taught me that my life was not an audition for the next life. Ellis taught me that family is important, but not at the risk of losing yourself. More importantly he taught me that I was worthy of having anything that I wanted in my life.
On September 9th 1971 Ellis wrote a list of demands for better living conditions for the inmates of Attica State Prison. The riots that

Poetic Recovery

followed claimed his life and the lives of officers and inmates alike. Ellis believed no man should have to live in prison under inhumane conditions and without dignity.

Life Don't Rhyme

L.D.

I CALLED HIM L.D.
I WAS YOUNG AND SILLY ENOUGH TO
BELIEVE HE WAS IN LOVE WITH ME.
MY HEAD REMAINED HIGH ABOVE THE CLOUDS
UP IN THE HEAVENS.
AFTER ALL HE WAS 18 AND I WAS 11
AFTER SCHOOL I HAD A PART TIME JOB, THE
REAL DEAL IS I GAVE L.D. EVERY DOLLAR I COULD
ROB
I BELIEVED THAT MONEY WOULD MAKE HIM
LOVE ME.
HOWEVER IT WAS NOT ME, THAT L.D. LOVED
THE MOST.
I FOUND OUT THE HARD WAY, IT WAS A BAG OF
DOPE.
AT MY AGE, MY FAMILIARITY WITH NARCOTICS
LEFT MUCH TO BE DESIRED.
SOON THEREAFTER FROM MY PART TIME JOB
I WAS FIRED.
AFTER ALL IS SAID AND DONE,
KNOWING THIS MAN BROUGHT RICHNESS AND
MEANING TO MY LIFE.
L.D. KNEW WHAT IT MEANT TO
FIGHT THE GOOD FIGHT.
IT WAS DURING OR PERHAPS AFTER THE
"ATTICA RIOTS"
THAT L.D. LOST HIS LIFE.
HE WAS MURDERED, BECAUSE HE TOOK A
STAND.
L.D. WROTE THE LIST OF DEMANDS.
TO ENABLE THOSE INCARCERATED IN PRISONS
THROUGHOUT THE UNITED STATES
TO HAVE A GRIEVANCE BOARD, SO THAT THE
DEATHS OF INMATES WILL NOT BE WRITTEN
OFF AS MISTAKES.

Poetic Recovery

Chapter Seventeen

After Ellis death, I continued to live with my mother and her husband in the house on Englert Street. It was near time for her to give birth to her sixth child, Allana. As always, life in the new house began calmly. Having been gone for almost a year from Dan and Arlene's home I had acquired some independence and some beliefs as to how I was going to prevent ending up unhappy, miserable and fearful like my mother. We were always at each other's throats, arguing, and forever angry. My escape route was high school. East High! My best friend was still Lettie. She lived in the neighborhood on Bay Street which made it convenient for her and I to spend even more time together.   Lettie's family always considered me as Ellis true girlfriend and I reveled in that feeling of belonging. While attending East High school I met, lied to, and dated an art teacher, King. Every chance I could manage to get out of my mother's house I would meet King. I was sexually active and uneducated about contraceptives, which only motivated me toward the library to read about how to avoid having children. After reviewing my mother's life, which I thought to be a fiasco, I re-signed myself to never having children. King and I developed a wonderful relationship. His family was warm, caring and thrilled that he was dating Shep's daughter. King's mother,
Ms.Ophelia often came by Shep's Paradise after

work with her girlfriends and enjoyed happy hour. King was a tall, brown skinned, hilariously funny and gifted artist. My mistake was not telling him the truth about my age. He discovered it when I offered to iron his shirts for work one Saturday afternoon while visiting my father. Well, Daddy intercepted King at the door with his shirts in tow. Daddy volunteered to tell him that I didn't iron my own clothes, yet alone those of a grown man. With that being said he added, "by the way did her fast ass tell you how old she is?" King yelled over his shoulder while walking briskly toward his car "Yeah, 17." Daddy of course responded "Well man, she lied!" "She is 12 years old!" I wanted to crawl under the porch of my father's house and die. For the rest of the day everyone had a great laugh at my expense. King left that day, but never left my life and for that I am blessed in having gained a true friend. Our walks to the airport in the snow accompanied by a bottle of Bali High, or Yago Sangria were utilized to teach me the importance of words, and the power they possess both spoken and written. However, that episode did not discourage me from lying about my age. I just decided to go all the way and make myself legal, and 18 was a great number. I successfully managed to complete the 8th grade but not without demonstrating my ability to forge my mother's name on her personal checks. Though Ellis was no longer in the picture I took a leap of faith and cashed a total of twelve hundred

Poetic Recovery

dollars in checks. I thought I could catch the mailman with the bank statement containing the returned checks before my mother. I was unsuccessful and she intercepted them first, having come home from work early that day. I was in the house with a man named Leroy who was also senior at East High school. Thank God for good hearing, because I was able to sneak Leroy out the side door of the Englert Street residence just in the nick of time. When Mommy confronted me about the checks, she was remarkably calm. I took this to be a sign that it would be in my favor to tell the truth. She informed me not to ask her to sign anymore report cards. She said "based on the signatures on these checks you are capable of signing my name better than me." She further informed me that when I began work that summer, every dime I made would go to repay my debt. I immediately thanked God, for having touched my mother's heart. More so for causing her to not beat fire out of my ass! This blessing inspired me to look for a job that would pay me enough money to repay my mother and keep my pockets filled. After all, being a freshman in high school was something I was looking forward to.

I was determined that my wardrobe would not be shabby, and more importantly, it would enhance the image I had been trying to portray since age ten, grown and sexy! At the age of twelve my job prospects were limited to baby-sitting, and I was not feeling that! I began to ask around about jobs to some of my friends who were coming home from college for the summer. They informed me that the city was hiring college students to tutor elementary school inner city children in reading, creative writing and math. I was certain I could pull this off as long as I could produce documents that verified I was in college and at least 18 years of age. Sure enough I got some help from my best friend Lettie. She didn't have to worry about a job because she had been working in the Plymouth Avenue pharmacy since the age of twelve, and had the hook up for speed. It was Lettie's genius that produced a resume, references and a New York State ID all of which were flawless. I was hired as a reading tutor for third graders. I was assigned a classroom, given supplies and fifteen students. My hours were 9am – 5pm Monday through Friday. The location was my old elementary School, PS.3, where I had gotten my head stuck between the building and the fence so many years earlier. I actually enjoyed that job because I knew I was gifted when it came to expressing my feelings on paper. Thanks to being the oldest child I knew how to interact with small children. They were eager to learn and very receptive to my method of teaching. By the time anyone got wise as to how old I really was, the summer was practically over, and I had paid my mother in full with a remainder of, three hundred dollars I had saved for school clothes. I still needed more money for

Poetic Recovery

the type of wardrobe I wanted to rock. I then took a job as a baby-sitter. There was a woman who worked for Rochester's Urban League who was in need of someone to watch her two young children five days a week. She hired me and I kept the job long enough to search the house and find a credit card to my favorite department store, Sibley's. Wouldn't you know my employer was also a regular patron of my daddy's bar. Well, I went shopping with the card for a couple of days buying the most stylish outfits of the season. On the second day as I was leaving the store, I remembered I needed stockings. As I attempted to pay for the stockings the cashier informed me that the card had been reported stolen. I immediately jumped into an Oscar winning performance and announced that there must be a mistake. I then inquired as to what floor the office was on in an effort to resolve the issue. The cashier informed me that I would have to go to the top floor, where I would find the credit department. I instructed her to keep my stockings behind the counter and that I would return as soon as I cleared up the matter. My heart was racing as fast as my legs were walking toward the nearest exit. Making it to the street, I breathed a sigh of relief when my knight in shining armor pulled up to the curb in a duce-and-a-quarter baby blue Buick and asked "want a ride?" I looked over my shoulder making sure I had not been followed out of the store by security, and looked up toward the heavens and said "Whew, thank you God!" Apparently a description was given to my employer, from whom I had stolen the card. She in turn informed my father of my latest caper. I was summoned to the bar that weekend and Daddy confronted me. Thanks to my grandma Lizzie I didn't walk into the fire on the blind, because she had given me a heads up, knowing full well that I was guilty. I would not risk lying to my Daddy, because he knew that I was the culprit and the repercussions would not have been in my favor. In a tone of voice that was unmistakable anger and disgust , Daddy said, "If you weren't my daughter I would put your fast ass in jail myself and you better be glad the lady was nice and reported the card as stolen and didn't have to pay for those clothes you bought." "Furthermore, if I had to pay her back a single dime, I would beat your ass until I get tired!"

      I realized that summer my criminal success had caused me to become more rebellious and confident in my skills of forgery. My parent's reaction to my behavior was to let me know that they loved me and were giving me enough rope to hang myself or until some judge decided to give me a jail sentence in some juvenile detention center. The summer was coming to a close and I wanted to end it with a bang. I had money, clothes and an extension on my life. My knight in shining armor was pushing the duce -and- a-quarter baby blue Buick was

Poetic Recovery

Enis. He was 23 years old and lived conveniently around the corner from my Daddy's house on Earl Street. Of course I had Enis under the assumption I was eighteen and in my last year of high school. I told him that I didn't want anyone in my business and that he should drop me off close to my home, but never in front of the house. Enis and I dated, but not exclusively. I was also seeing a car dealer named Willy. He had a car dealership on East Main Street not far from East High School. He was married which ensured he would be silent about our relationship. There was no doubt in my mind that if my Daddy found out I was involved a married man he would hit the roof and kill Willy. It was the end of the summer and that kind of drama I would avoid at all cost.

Life Don't Rhyme

Chapter Eighteen

    I met Willy while working in my father's bar one weekend. He was one of the customers who spoke to me longer than usual in addition to slipping me his phone number. We had to be very careful about our meetings. Willy's wife worked in a bank and made sure that he always had money when selling used cars wasn't going so well. Enis on the other hand was just eye candy and served as a nice touch to be in the company of, more importantly he was single with a car. That summer Enis invited me to a wedding the last weekend in August. I asked my mother for permission to attend the wedding. She granted my request and told me I was to be in the house by midnight. She also made a point of telling me that somebody's mother had better call her and assure her I would be given a ride home. I called my best friend Lettie and told her to pretend to be somebody's mother and to tell my mother that she would be responsible for my returning home. With that little task out of the way I informed Enis where he would be picking me up that Saturday. This was the first wedding I had ever attended with a date. On the day of the wedding I made sure that I was undeniably cute. I wore a turquoise mini floral sleeveless sheath with a high collar, flat patent leather kiwi green baby doll slippers embellished with a bow and matching clutch purse. My hair was short and curly, with not a hair out of place. Green hoop

Poetic Recovery

earrings from the famous Woolworth's novelty store put the finishing touch on the outfit.

The ceremony was romantic, and heartfelt and the reception was at an all time high. The music was banging and the food delicious. I drank champagne and Dewar's White Label Scotch with a splash of club soda. I was feeling no pain and Enis took my condition as the perfect opportunity to seduce me. We went from the reception straight to the motel. What ever happened between Enis and I that night, was certainly consentual. As daylight crept into the motel room I realized I had not made my curfew. We left the motel at 5am. It didn't matter where Enis dropped me off at that time in the morning, because I knew my fate was sealed the moment I walked in the door of my mother's house. I made it clear to Enis that I would not be available to see him again for awhile. I explained to him that I had to go out of town and would contact him when I returned. We kissed good night and I took my shoes off and ran around the corner home. I attempted to put the key into the lock as quietly as possible. There was no need, because my mother opened the door for me. What she said next scared me more than what she intended to do to me. That morning I re-named my mother Shirley Holmes.

Life Don't Rhyme

For My Mother aka Shirley Holmes

Shirley Holmes was the greatest detective known only to her children.
I called her Shirley Holmes though she was Mommy to me.
I can still hear her asking "what time did I say be home"?
"Take your brothers and sisters with you
You ain't grown'!"
"'You will not leave my house looking like a tramp"
"Alright I am tired of talking, go get my strap."
"Oh you want to forge checks, do you?
"Get yourself a summer job.
You're going to pay me back for those checks you forged".
"Sign your report card!" "For what?"
"You write my name better than me"
"Slow down princess, please, please, please."
"Zoe, please come home."
"The street is nowhere for a child alone."
"I love you princess because you are me."
"I am trying to recover our relationship called We."
"It is not that I am nosey or Inspector Gadget either.
"It is because I am your mother you'll never get a breather."

Poetic Recovery

She said "I am going beat your ass, because you seem to have convinced yourself that you are grown." She was still pregnant with her sixth child and informed me that my ass whooping could wait because she was going to get some more sleep so as to have enough strength to wear my ass out. Until then she instructed me to find something she could beat me with since I was already awake. That was my cue to leave and begin living my life on my own. I had some money saved up and another man waiting in the wings to assist me with the move. By the time school started I had my own apartment and was attending school as a freshman as scheduled. I made my father and mother aware that I was fine and that they should not worry about me and by all means to stop looking for me. I didn't understand just how stupid I sounded telling my parents not worry about me until I got older. On September 11th 1970 I saw my mother again. She was in the hospital about to give birth to her sixth child, my sister Allana. The hospital staff was preparing her for a spinal tap when I walked into her room. Her facial expression confirmed she was in a great deal of pain. She told me she was glad I was well and that I continued to attend school. Then she said what I had been waiting for years to hear. She had finally made up her mind and was leaving her husband. She told me she couldn't stay married to her asshole of a husband any longer, and explained how the relationship was taking its toll out on her mental health. She ended our conversation by telling me

Life Don't Rhyme

she was going to move to New York City and asked if I would be interested in coming with her. We agreed right there in that hospital room that when she actually made that move I would join her, but until then I would do what I had to for myself alone! Though my mother attempted many times to summon the strength to leave her husband this time was different. I could hear the urgency in her voice. I could also feel the pain from the years she had been content to be dragged through a relationship that brought nothing but pain, suffering and fear. When I turned to leave the hospital room I kissed her and told her to stay in touch. I felt a twinge of guilt believing that I had deserted my siblings. I quickly rid myself of that baggage, realizing that there was nothing that I could actually take responsibility for other than myself and my own actions. I still had faith in knowing that God takes care of babies and fools so I knew we all were covered.

Poetic Recovery

Without a Man

Sometime during the sixties,
Between "Say It Loud I'm Black and I'm
Proud" and "We Shall Overcome."
Mommy married a white a man.
I was 9 or 10 I guess
I kept asking God "Is this some kind of test?"
I realized soon after the marriage
That mommy was scared and afraid.
I heard the cruel and nasty things he'd say.
I watched him hit her and make her cry.
I swore alone in my room
I would hate him til I died.
Mommy remained married to him
To give their marriage try after try
He told her that he would change
I knew it was a lie.
Just like clockwork the terror began
He hit my Mommy again and again.
This time Mommy said get all the kids out of the house.
I did as I was told, and got my brothers and myself out.
No I cannot lie she went back again
It took her longer to discover
She could make it without a man.

Life Don't Rhyme

Chapter Nineteen

    The discovery of my mother being able to make it without a man came about during the Fall of 1970. Mommy stayed true to her word and, more importantly to herself. She was now living in New York City. She had been living there for a couple of months prior to sending for me to come and join her. She had once again entrusted my brothers and sisters to the care of Nana. All I could do was pray for Darien, Brandon, Rachelle and Allana. Mommy hoped to send for them within the next year. My brother Kenan refused to live with Nana and went to live with our father instead.

    I flew into La Guardia airport where mommy met me with a male friend. She introduced him as Romaine. Romaine was a distinguished older man who stood 5' 3". He was a singer and piano player in an upscale restaurant and piano bar in midtown Manhattan called Jack's Pier 52. I could sense from the moment I met him he too was another one of my mother's mistakes. His eyes roamed my body, the way a pedophile scans the playground for an innocent child. I did not want to intrude upon my mother's happiness, and I went out of my way not to lead this man on. But my thinking told me I had to look out for myself and my mother. My young mind also told me if I was going to get fucked, I was also going to do the fucking.

Poetic Recovery

My mother was renting a room in Harlem on 133rd Street and Seventh Avenue in the home of an elderly woman, Mrs. Kimp. It was clean and we shared the bathroom and kitchen. We could have been in a cave for all I cared. What was important was that my mother and I were together. She enrolled me into an all girl's high school, Washington Irving off of 16th Street near Union Square where I continued classes in the 9th grade. Staying true to form I was dressed in a black and beige tweed suit with flat beige ballet slippers, and for effect I also wore top and bottom false eye lashes. My hair was cut short in an Afro and I knew I was cute. I realized how old I looked when one of the teachers mistook me for a teacher. My decisions concerning my appearance were starting to be noticed. I rationalized that this was the effect I was desperately searching for. My mother and I left the house most mornings together, she to work and I to school; however I returned home alone. Once I conquered the New York subway system I was able to travel with ease. I avoided the girls I went to school with because they acted immature. I quickly made friends with two females who lived in my neighborhood, in the St. Nicholas Housing Projects which spans from 127th Street to 131st street. My new friends Arian and Doretta would serve to enlighten me about the new lifestyle I was about to embark upon.

Chapter Twenty

Arian was a single mother with two children. She lived with her parents and older sister Cheron. Arian was 5' 4" tall, short brown hair, smooth brown skin and beautiful brown almond shaped eyes. They were her best feature and she utilized them to capture the hearts of her male suitors. Arian was people conscious always making sure to be seen with the right people. She would go out of her way to make sure she was never seen with the wrong ones. I soon found out it was because she was also married. She loved her children and went to any lengths to provide for them. Arian's mother was the mainstay in her family though her father was also in the home, Arians mother was the rock. She doted on her grandchildren as well as her daughters. She worked long hours in an effort to relocate her family to Queens and out of the projects where they began life as a family so many years before. Arian's family was a prime example of the lengths parents will go, to create better lives for their children.

My other new friend Doretta was 5' 8" tall and slender, with smooth chocolate skin. Her face was oval shaped with sincere brown eyes that told you she was a no-nonsense type of woman. She too lived with her mother, Mina. Mina was strength personified. Her children were her life and she loved them unconditionally. Doretta's mother was fond of Newports, coffee, pound cake and Pepsi. No matter who you were

Poetic Recovery

if you knocked on the door of apartment 5A you were sure to be offered something, not excluding a place to sleep. Doretta was a single parent with two children at the time we met. She was in relationship with a hustler who adored her, Jamar. Both women were accustomed to having men in their lives that were generous with money. This being true, it made sense that having them as friends would eventually lead me to the same type of man. It would be Doretta, who would introduce me to just the man I was looking for. I made it a point to walk home from the subway through St. Nicholas Projects daily after school. There was an area in the Projects called the circle where guys would hang out everyday sitting on the benches, selling drugs, drinking liquor, smoking weed, playing chess and talking shit to the girls seeking attention. I knew that was where I was going to find someone to love me, and rescue my mother and I from the one room accommodations we currently occupied.

    His name was Jerome, his friends called him Rome. I was walking through the circle from school one afternoon purposely dressed in a green kilt and matching cape. I wore Nine West penny loafers and forest green tights. Rome had been clocking me coming the same route ever since Doretta had introduced us. It was a cold Fall day and he took this opportunity to wave me over to where he and his friends were serving customers. He introduced me to a couple of his

Life Don't Rhyme

friends Yusef, and Flats. They were polite and offered me some of the joint they were passing around. I refused wanting to make a good first impression. I succeeded, because at that moment Rome told them if he wanted me to have a joint he would give it to me. He gave me a cup of Blackberry brandy instead and directed me to where I should sit until he concluded his business. He began the conversation by telling me he had recently come home from prison for selling drugs, and was currently on parole. Rome was 6' tall with skin the color of dark brown clay. He had the facial features of an Indian chief, sexy brown eyes complete with a sharp jaw line and a pointy nose. He was soft spoken, in a way that let you know he could become volatile if angered.

  My first question was did he use his product which was heroin. He answered "no not anymore." I was relieved by his answer. I don't know what it was about Rome that made me believe him, but I did. We talked and I told him that I was in high school. He was cool with that, which was a relief. Rome was seven years my senior, which was what drew me to him in addition to his being generous. Every day I stopped to see him on my way home from school, he would give me money, take me to dinner or the movies. I bought something new to wear every day. My mother didn't question me or she was so tired from working she let it go knowing that the truth would surface eventually. I

Poetic Recovery

believe she didn't question me because she knew there would be nothing she could say to reverse my actions. One day in particular I met Rome, he told me he was broke and didn't have any money. He informed me he needed to report to his parole officer right away. Then he asked me if he could borrow twenty dollars, and that he would repay me the following day. At first I was hesitant about giving him some money. Then I thought to myself, he just gave you one hundred and fifty dollars yesterday let's see if he keeps his word. So I gave him the money and watched as he jumped into a cab. Something told me I had made the right decision and a great investment. The next day as I came out of school, there standing across the street in front of the pizza shop on Irving Place was Rome. What he did and said next touched my heart. He handed me three one hundred dollar bills and one twenty dollar bill and said "I don't like to owe anyone, not even my woman." I took him straight to meet my mother. We concocted a lie, telling her that he was a student in college and worked part time in sales for an import-export company. Rome sold heroin! What was true, was that it was imported from Vietnam and exported throughout the streets of Harlem and beyond. I never inquired as to who his supplier was. Names like Frank Lucas and Nicky Barnes could be overheard in many of his conversations with his crew. Eventually I would come in close contact with both gentlemen. Shortly after the

Life Don't Rhyme

introduction Rome contributed to my mother's move, out of that one room walk up, into an apartment in East Harlem on Pleasant Avenue. I never ever discussed sex with my mother after the incident with my stepfather. I believed no one had the right to tell me anything concerning who I gave my body to. My sexual activity was an unspoken given. I strongly suspect I confirmed her suspicions about my being sexually active, because I often spent nights in a hotel with Rome only to come home early in the morning to change clothes for school. I was taking birth control pills because I was serious about not bring any unwanted children into my life. Realizing how much money Rome and I wasted going to the hotel I convinced her that it would be cheaper and advantageous to her if she let Rome move in with me until we could save enough money to get our own apartment. I told her she would then be able to send for my brothers and sisters who were still living in Rochester with Nana. My mother allowed Rome and I to live together because she wanted me close to her and knowing that I was safe was her priority. Rome taught me a lot about the sale and distribution of heroin. I learned how to cut it, bag it and tag it. The one thing he forbade me to do was make a sale or skip school. This meant the only money I was privy to was what he gave me, and that was a problem! I didn't like having to ask anyone for anything not even my man.

Poetic Recovery

Chapter Twenty One

I was fortunate to find a female with whom I went to school who appeared to be into a lot more than the classes we attended. Her name was Jamie. I was sniffing cocaine in the school bathroom in between classes when she asked for a blow. I offered her some so as to break the ice. When she accepted I confirmed that the ice had been broken. I gave her just enough cocaine to get her relaxed enough to tell me about herself. She confided in me that she had a Sugar Daddy who kept her laced with clothes and cash. She said he was a White man who owned a chain of grocery stores in Harlem. She informed me that he paid a lot of money for young black girls to model lingerie and he paid a minimum of five hundred dollars depending on the services performed. I can tell you I jumped at the opportunity to make a connection like that. It would be my own extra income and wouldn't require more than an hour of my time. I immediately told Jamie to set up a date that same week.

Sol was a short Jewish man with an imagination that was out of this world. He owned the Frontier Supermarket chain throughout Harlem. All it took was the first meeting where I dazzled him as if I was on the set of a major porno film. After that I saw him regularly once a week after school with Jamie for six months straight. She and I would play with each other in knee socks, white panties and bras while Sol hid in the closet. Sol bought brand new lingerie for us to model in for every date. I made him aware that I was open to solo dates, if he was open to providing an increase in pay. Our relationship lasted for years, well after I graduated from high school. Once I turned twenty-one I became his recruiter.

      Our relationship would span three decades and include family members and many of my close girlfriends who I knew would and could, provide sexual services without any fuss. My role was to book the dates and of course pay the participants. Throughout my sophomore, and junior year in high school I did nothing except go to school, count, and spend money lavishly. Of course scheduling dates for Sol had become a lucrative source of income that afforded me more things than Rome could provide at times. With Rome getting arrested regularly, I always needed to have large amounts of money on hand as a retainer for our lawyer. Those cases were always thrown out because of a law known as illegal search and seizure. These arrests became a regular occurrence, and I used them to establish my own clientele among Rome's regular customers who knew I was his woman. Rome never stayed in jail longer than overnight. However when the Rockefeller law became active it rocked my world and the worlds of many other people. Hustlers began to go to prison and people we dealt with regularly began dying or

Poetic Recovery

telling on other colleagues who were in the dope game. Rome was no exception. One bust that took place in my mother's house on Pleasant Avenue cofirmed for my mother what business Rome was truly in. It was common practice for me to smoke half a joint before
leaving for school in the mornings, and leave the remainder in the ashtray for Rome when he awakened. Rome had an excruciating toothache the night before the bust. He had taken several Tylenol with codeine, in addition to drinking straight shots of Tangueray gin and an ample amount of cocaine. Little did we know, the tenants on the first floor were also selling weight in heroin. Living in Harlem always made you a candidate for robbery. That day someone decided to rob all the apartments on the C-side of the building, where my mother, Rome, and I shared the apartment. Rome was knocked out in a cold sleep and was not aware that anyone had entered the apartment, that is until the police arrived and found him asleep with a joint in the ashtray and about twelve bundles of heroin under the nightstand. He was arrested, arraigned and released. That would be his last pass in the courts under the illegal search and seizure law. All future busts would come under the heading of the Rockefeller Law.

My relationship with Rome wasn't all about selling dope and going to jail. I took great pride in introducing him to things of culture below 110th Street that is. Before me, Rome limited his

Life Don't Rhyme

leisure activities to 125th Street, the Apollo and the many clothing stores that lined both sides of this historic street. Rome being a lover of jazz had never attended a live concert at Lincoln Center. Knowing this whenever any jazz artist performed I bought tickets. We attended concerts at Carnegie Hall, Madison Square Garden, and Radio City Music Hall. We went to the Village for late night dinners and jazz sets at the Blue Note. We would visit
museums and art exhibits. We shopped on 5th and Madison Avenues and I rented limousines on special occasion, and bought him jewelry in the 47th Street Diamond District. We attended plays, and anything else I could think of that was away from St. Nicholas Projects. Rome never denied me anything and never squabbled about how much money I spent. I felt like a tour guide introducing a little boy to a brand new world a world we enjoyed together.

    It was the end of my junior year when Rome and I finally moved out of my mother's apartment and into our own on 93rd Street and Second Avenue. My mother stayed true to her word and sent for all of her children to come to New York except for my brother Kenan who continued to live with our father. Darien was in junior high school, and Brandon, Rachelle and Allana were attending elementary school. Rome and I took on the responsibility of providing money for our families regularly. Rome's mother was caring for his nephews in lieu of the death of his sister. It is difficult to be all things to all people, but that never stopped Rome. He often would decline going on vacations so that he could stay and sell dope, just so my mother and his would have the things they wanted and needed. Rome helped me to sponsor a much needed vacation for my mother and her girlfriend to Jamaica. Since her arrival in New York she had been working long hours. She had never taken time out to enjoy a real vacation since she had begun having children. I was glad to be in position to send her on this trip no matter where the money came from. Rome and I made sure that no one we loved went without.

    The inevitable finally happened and Rome got busted for the umpteenth time. He was sentenced to 3-6 years. I was now totally on my own. I knew there was no turning back and I had to show and prove that I was capable of holding down my own life and the lives of the people I had taken responsibility for. Rome always had me put everything in my name, should any questions arise when posting bail. However with him away I was responsible for taking care of all my bills. Thankfully we had furnished the apartment before he went to prison. With him away things would be tight. Now was the time when I would utilize all the things I was taught and had witnessed during my relationship with Rome. Throughout High School I had always kept a legal job but I soon realized that money wouldn't be enough to cover my expenses. Welfare was not an option. I swore years ago when my mother had to endure that part of the system that I would do whatever was necessary in order to avoid being a Welfare recipient. I also had another major unexpected surprise, I was pregnant. I didn't know until another man, my current barber informed me while ferociously sucking on my breast that they were lactating. I informed my mother of my condition and made it very clear that under no circumstances was I going to have a child. I asked that she sign the necessary papers for the hospital so that I could receive an immediate abortion. Surprisingly enough there was no discussion. I wouldn't have listened anyway. I knew the child was Rome's however it was my body and I was not having anyone's child broke! I had sense enough to know the direction in which my life was headed there was no room for a baby. There was no emotion in my decision to rid myself of what I believed would be an intrusion on my life. What's more important is that I did a quick review of my childhood which confirmed my decision to be a "no-brainer."

What I recall about that episode in my life is that, it was brief! The decision to abort was no more significant to me than deciding what color lingerie I would coordinate with my daily attire. I had no regrets, dreams or nervous breakdowns as a result of this decision, nor do I have any now. Zoe means life, and if I had to part with a life to have a life then so be it.

Chapter Twenty Two

Enter "Pimp's Palace." Needing a job and being a Senior in high school didn't leave a whole lot of options as to where I could work and get the kind of money I needed or was use to in order to maintain the lifestyle to which I had become accustomed. I was committed to graduating from high school. The number one reason being my Daddy told me if I didn't make a change in my life I would end up a High School dropout, pregnant, and on welfare. Well I knew it was up to me to make sure he ate those words. Daddy's ulterior motive in saying this was to make sure I did the exact opposite. It also occurred to me I could continue to sell heroin since Rome had acquired a loyal clientele. However the problem was his partners would all want something in return. This would put Rome's existing friendships at risk. Hustler's took pride being able to say they got a piece of ass from a man's girl while he was locked up. I refused to play myself like that. My solution was to sell dope with one exception I would buy my own. That was easy enough and I could sell it at my leisure to a select few people I knew only bought bundles of twenty five dollar bags. A customer also gave me a number to call about a job as a barmaid in an afterhour's club. I had never worked in an establishment other than my father's that sold liquor. I figured it couldn't be that difficult to pour up shots and talk shit for tips so I interviewed for the job. I wore a short skirt and an equally short afro. I thought I must have been impressive because the man who interviewed me hired me right there on the spot. Boy, oh boy, was I naive!

    The club was in a duplex located on Manhattan's Upper West Side on Columbus Avenue and 81st street. It was directly across the street from the Museum of Natural History. The club offered a plush atmosphere that catered to the leisurely activities of pimps, prostitutes, con players, and of course drug dealers. My job description consisted of nothing more than serving top shelf liquor to those patrons who sniffed cocaine, heroin, or smoked weed. There was another hot commodity that sold very well to the working girls. It was speed in the form of a pill called Cycos. My bosses made sure we had plenty on hand. These little pills were also an investment for the pimps. When taken they kept the working girls working, high and wide awake.

    I learned there were particular Avenues in the city that the girls who worked the streets, used to pick up dates. These areas were called "the stroll or the track." If the girls worked the pimps made money and spent it at the Pimps Palace. Realizing the potential wealth of this business I put my best friends down with becoming employed as barmaids. Arian and Doretta were uptown girls and were in no way interested in giving any man any money,

Poetic Recovery

at anytime for anything especially a pimp. We served liquor and drugs and nothing else for a minute that is. The tips were good most nights and as barmaids we learned how to steal to make them better. I learned quickly that my afro was not acceptable in an atmosphere where hair defined your status. I began wearing wigs as did Doretta and Arian. Our tips immediately increased. I always had a quick tongue and a way with words. It was behind the bar of Pimp's Palace where I utilized my gift to gab from morning till dawn. Mostly I talked shit and stroked egos. Through all of this I still managed to leave the club in time for my first period class and stay awake throughout the day with the help of some good cocaine. I also had a second job after school as a receptionist in a Black Cultural Center called the House of Kuumba located on Lenox Avenue and 112th street. I left that job at 9pm went to my apartment and slept until 1am. I would get up, dress and report to work by 2am. I kept this schedule throughout the remainder of my senior year in high school. Under no circumstances was I going to allow anything to interfere with my graduating from high school on time.

Life Don't Rhyme

Chapter Twenty Three

I learned immediately that women in this lifestyle were required to have a man. Pimp's were always asking Doretta, Arian and I when we were going to choose. Choosing was a common term used when a woman gave her earnings to one man exclusively. This was a very serious step in the life of any woman who was a prostitute, con player, or drug seller. All men below 110th street considered themselves pimps, and could have many women each performing a different job function. Some of our patrons used the fact that we didn't have a man as an excuse not to give us tips. This issue had to be resolved and I had figured out just the way to resolve it.

The pimp social circle was a very close knit group of some of the most handsome, articulate and intelligent men I had ever laid eyes on. There was also an equal amount of loud, garish, and ignorant pimps as well. They had names like Love, Diamond, Flash, and of course the most common Redd. For the most part they were all gentlemen to an extent. The real pimps had legitimate business dealings independent of the income they received from their women. The original "Gentlemen of Leisure" never depended on any one woman to give them money to live. When a woman did choose she performed her job function, whether it was going into the banks, selling drugs, or

Poetic Recovery

selling pussy with the professionalism that insured her position with her man. The bottom line is, no matter her task she would bring her entire "bankroll" or "trap" home and give it to the man she wanted to be with. If she belonged to another pimp he in turn would go to the last man she was with and make him aware that she had chosen and now belonged to him. Very often this exchange of ladies did not go smoothly. The two gentlemen who owned the "Pimp's Palace" were Jerry and Billy. They were intelligent, handsome, impeccably groomed, charming, and ruthless. Jerry was a gambler who liked the horses, cee-low, craps and anything you could bet on in addition to an attraction to Stetson hats. Billy on the other hand was laid back, and deadly serious about getting money, from all sources. I soon learned that Billy was uninhibited regarding anything that provided pleasure for him and those he deemed worthy. He was always properly attired resembling a dapper Wall Street stock broker.

    Both men protected their women and that included the bar maids and they both trusted me. I was given the keys and put in charge of hiring and firing of barmaids, the opening and closing of the spot, and making sure the bar was always fully stocked. I also suggested they rig the juke box so that you could hear one song for a quarter, where normally you would hear two. I sold plain soda and juice with plenty of ice for two dollars a glass. Needless to say that was money I always kept for myself. I took advantage of the numerous opportunities that presented themselves in the form of a discreet way to make extra money. I rarely made a move without discussing it first with my employers. Jerry and Billy were always ready to tell me the real deal on each and every customer who propositioned me. Of course, being young, the old adage a hard head makes a soft ass played out on a couple of occasions. Once a "drag boy" aka con man from Alabama offered me a thousand dollars for a date. I skipped school and took him to my house. He actually let me count the money before he placed it in the envelope after which he pulled the old switch-a-roo. That was so embarrassing. Upon discovery of having been tricked, I went to shop for a hat to wear to work that same night. When he arrived to the club he refused to let me serve him a drink. That is until I bought him a drink and took my hat off to him thanking him for showing me a game that no other living person would be able to play on me again. After that he was my best customer and tipped me well whenever he would take a "sting". I had another close call while engaged in a photo shoot with another couple, for which I was paid. Little did I know Jerry's wife Blondine had organized a threesome in an effort to belittle me in front of her husband and the patrons of Pimp's Palace. Jerry had an ulterior motive and retrieved every Polaroid and explained to me, if I was going to seek his advice then I had better

Poetic Recovery

begin to take it. He went on to say no woman allows nude pictures to be taken of herself unless she gets the negatives and far more cash than I had accepted.

Billy on the other hand was always down to earths except when he was portraying a Mack with no cheese. Billy was serious about his money and very professional when it came to his business dealings no matter if he were conducting business with a male or female. It was because of this rare quality I remained in his good graces. I never really cared whether or not a man ever trusted me, before Billy. There was something about him that told me if he could trust me I would be his friend for life, and he would be mine. I was so right.

One day my friend Arian and I were having a discussion about "choosing." We decided if we were going to choose, it may as well be the men we worked for. Arian was talking to Billy and I was talking to Jerry. They both knew I had a man who was in prison. Such trivial matters did not concern either man, they thrived on competition. Jerry and Billy made a point of telling me that because my man Rome was from Harlem he was not going accept his woman's new career change working around pimps and selling pussy. I took on the attitude that what he doesn't know won't hurt him. One night Arian and I decided to give selling pussy a try on what was known as the stroll. We began the evening with dinner and drinks to boost our courage. Any square would have thought we were going to real jobs. Half drunk, we then bought two yo-yo's that lit up in the dark and proceeded to walk to Park Avenue near the Waldorf-Astoria hotel. We approached several men walking alone and struck up conversations with one liner's such as "hey baby, you want a date?" or "going out handsome?" We didn't get one encouraging response. We were quickly running low on courage and our self esteem was fading fast. We decided to go into the hotel's rear entrance and have another drink at the bar. Just as we were about to enter through the revolving doors of the Waldorf, New York's finest invited us into the back seat of their patrol car. We were immediately whisked away, read our rights, charged, arrested, photographed and fingerprinted. We were taken to Central Booking located at 100 Centre Street where we waited for desk appearance tickets. With all the chaos going on around me I remembered I had the keys to Pimp's Palace on me and would not be able to open the club at two o'clock as was my job. I made the call to inform Jerry and Billy of mine and Arian's great adventure. Upon our release we both returned to the Pimp's Palace at 6 o'clock that morning. We were laughed at, and labeled "the blind leading the blind." I had heard of call girl services and understood now why they were so successful. Billy had a couple of girls that worked exclusively from their apartments. I made a mental note to discuss with him how I

Poetic Recovery

could begin my own call girl service as soon as this episode stopped being the hot topic of every pimp's conversation who frequented the spot. It would be quite some time before I would venture back to selling pussy on the streets.

    I continued going to High School and graduated on time. I also began a lucrative call girl service from my apartment complete with two phones; one for dates and one for friends and family. I knew back then my lifestyle would continue to be unsavory so I refused to take pictures for my High School year book. I believed the pictures in the year book would enable law enforcement to track me down if and when the time arose and I became wanted. In my mind it would be one less picture to identify me. So to pacify my mother I rented a cap and gown and took some pictures for her and my daddy. I notified Washington Irving High School of my decision not to attend the graduation ceremony instructing them to put my high school diploma in the mail.

Life Don't Rhyme

Chapter Twenty Four

When Rome was released from prison I picked him up from Fishkill Correctional facility in a limousine. I gave him one thousand dollars in $100 bills. I had Arian's friend Benny who was a jeweler make him a beautiful gold and diamond ring in the shape of a ram's head because he was an Aries. He was pleased I had been able to maintain our apartment with his belongings intact. He eventually discovered just what I had been doing since his incarceration.

It wasn't hard to figure out, since I had two phones and only allowed him to answer one. Just as Jerry and Billy had predicted Rome was devastated. It was his ego that suffered most. He discovered I didn't need him anymore and from there we separated. He remained in the 93rd street apartment until he was evicted and returned to St. Nicholas Projects where his mother still lived with his two nephews. Out of necessity I did "choose" Jerry as my man. He set me up in an apartment on the 27th floor of an apartment building called Carnegie Towers on East 87th Street between Lexington and Park Avenues. The address alone was one of prestige. It meant I had finally made it to the big time, but at what cost?

I had an exclusive clientele made up of lawyers, doctors, stock brokers, hustlers and of course pimps. Yes, pimps! They were big tricks who swore me to secrecy if I wanted to continue getting their money. However my main source of income was selling cocaine and managing the Pimps Palace. The Pimp's Palace was doing great business, though we were frequently visited by the local precinct police for financial donations to their favorite charity, them! Jerry liked to gamble on sports, so I began patronizing professional heavy weight boxing matches, namely those in which Muhammad Ali and Joe Frazier fought. I went to Super Bowls and NBA championship games. My purpose in attending these events was to sell cocaine. I found that I often made more money at these events than I did when working in the afterhours spot. Arian and Doretta continued to work in the Pimp's Palace and often spent time in my new apartment sniffing cocaine, drinking cognac and talking about our men.

    One Saturday morning around 5 o'clock one of the busiest nights of the week, the police decided they needed a bust, and Pimp's Palace was it. We made the front page of the *Daily News* and received television coverage. Arian and I were the barmaids working that night. Doretta had called out sick. We used the same names we used during our arrest on Park Avenue. She was Sally Matthews and I was Ellen Kendrick It was the only time in my life I can actually say that I enjoyed being in jail. My mother heard about the bust having watched the news. The publicity came about due to the overwhelming complaints from the neighbors concerning the amount of cars and traffic going in and out of "The Pimp's Palace". It was a residential neighborhood that frowned upon on the business of white slavery, not to mention selling narcotics. We were arrested, read our rights, charged, booked, photographed and fingerprinted again and ultimately forced to shut down for a minute. The moment we were all released from jail we returned to the spot only to be greeted by broken glass, wasted liquor and many packages of overlooked narcotics.

      Billy was aggravated because we had been hit hard that night in addition to taking a very large personal loss in product. It was this night I learned the dangers of what happens to a woman when she tells a pimp to kiss her ass. Billy having been locked up all day had asked that his women not bother him with their petty bickering. All were compliant except Ellen from Chicago. She chose to extend that deadly invitation of her body part to Billy and he did indeed accept. The whipping I witnessed proved to be a lesson and a source of encouragement toward what words to never say to anyone.

      Though we re-opened, business was never quite the same. The cash flow was heavily impacted by the constant presence of New York's finest. Jerry was exploring other venues for relocation; in addition to feeding his gambling addiction from the meger profits we were taking in. Shortly after the first police invasion Billy returned to his home in Cleveland Ohio. His

Poetic Recovery

main woman Diane was about to give birth to their son. Shortly after the birth of their son a home invasion proved fatal and Billy was shot and his woman murdered. My heart was wounded at the news of this heinous crime. I prayed for Billy's survival and I am forever grateful to God for sparing the lives of Billy and his son.

Jerry on the other hand proved not to be a good partner and chose this time of loss to gamble any and all profits made in the Pimps Palace during Billy's absence. I continued to keep a daily record of the clubs profits and report them to Billy. The moment Billy returned we had a homecoming that can best be described as the hottest party in town. Jerry's demonstration of disrespect dissolved all business dealings between the two. Billy never let on to anyone that I had made him aware of how grimy his partner had become concerning their business. I continued to remain with Jerry, though it was only for self profit, and nothing more. I robbed Jerry every chance I got. As for giving him my money, that would never happen. I still had a need to chase the almighty dollar and every dollar I caught was mine.

Life Don't Rhyme

Let The Games Begin

Chapter Twenty Five

In return for graduating from high school my mother gave me an all expense paid trip to London England. However, I utilized the trip to purchase those magic little pills called Cycos the pimps fed to their girls to keep them productive. I took advantage of being a tourist while I was there and remained for an entire month. During my visit I met a woman who owned a bed and breakfast. There were several young women who also rented rooms. One took a particular liking to me because I was from New York. She told me she enjoyed the city while on assignment for a photo shoot in a major magazine. My habit of searching area's that were not privy to me prevailed and I lucked up and found some exquisite jewelry belonging to some of the guest. On the day of my departure from London I carefully removed those items I thought were genuine and of worth and hightailed it to Heathrow Airport in route back to New York. I hadn't thought for a moment that the items I had stolen would be missed as quickly as they were. Upon my arrival at Kennedy Airport I was met by security. For some unforeseen reason, I stashed the jewelry in the only cavity of my body I knew no one would check, I was right. Sure enough I was strip searched and relieved of several items of clothing I had not declared. I was then given a receipt for those items. Luckily enough the 250,000 pills I purchased at .35 a pill were

Life Don't Rhyme

hidden in the bottom of a cage where a cute Scottish Terrier I purchased upon my arrival in London was comfortably sleeping. I had the dog shipped prior to my departure so that it could be given its shots and papers. This insured a prompt and uneventful arrival, at least for the dog and the pills. The business deal between Jerry and I was very profitable each pill sold for ten dollars. I knew who I was dealing with and had sense enough to retrieve fifty thousand of those little beauties for my own personal profit. I gave Jerry back his initial investment for the pills and we split the remaining profit not equally but close enough for me not to have to return to work unless I wanted to. Business in The Pimp's Palace had become very slow and the only source of income was the sale of cocaine and pills.

     The police continued to visit the club and demand money on a regular basis. The money never quite flowed as it once did. It was during this time I realized the things I was doing to achieve independence were still keeping me held hostage to someone. I just couldn't give Jerry any money hell I certainly wasn't giving him any of mine. It was against everything my daddy taught me and Jerry had become too demanding. So we parted and I kept the Park Avenue apartment. Surprisingly enough he was ok with my decision to move on. The fact remained that the rent was due and I had to get busy. Rome to the rescue! I found him right

Poetic Recovery

where I met him in St. Nicholas Projects. I moved him into the Park Avenue apartment with me and he was pleased to be there. We enjoyed each other's company and began to enjoy life together again. It didn't last because Rome had begun smoking Angel Dust which caused him to lose more product than he sold and money. There were times I'd receive phone calls in the middle of the night from some of the guys he hung out with, telling me he had awaken somewhere and couldn't remember how he had gotten there. In most instances he had been robbed of everything of value. I couldn't contend with him smoking the Angel Dust. I needed more money than he was able to bring to the table and continuing to be with Rome was in no way going to be advantageous. His smoking of Angel Dust had become a liability. I truly loved Rome. He was a good man and very good to me and my family. He treated me as if I were royalty and insisted that I never allow anyone to treat me otherwise. He placed me on a pedestal, forgetting that I was a human being and not his prize possession to be paraded around on his arm like a show piece. Lack of income caused me to move out of the Park Avenue apartment, into Rome's mother's apartment along with his two nephews. Rome's mother, Miss.Vy as everyone called her genuinely loved the fact that I was with her son. She too saw the change in him as a result of smoking Angel Dust and the change in me.

Life Don't Rhyme

Though she never passed judgment concerning my activities she let me know she was aware that I was not the same young woman her son introduced to her years earlier. She confided in me that his behavior under the influence of the Angel Dust frightened her. She had no problem in letting me know that she felt a source of comfort having me live in her home. Rome's love affair with Angle Dust had taken priority over our relationship and the people who loved him. I understood I couldn't rely on him for financial support and the effect Angel Dust had over Rome caused me to worry. He and I both had some friends who had taken their own lives by jumping from the top floor of a couple of buildings in the Projects, as a result of smoking Angel Dust. It had taken over 123rd Street and Seventh Avenue. This area was primarily known for selling quality marijuana however, when Angel Dust came on the scene, good weed took a back seat. Oh, I didn't pass judgment on the consumers of Dust before I tried it. From what I remember I smoked a joint on a summer's day outside in the back of Rome's building. I sat on the bench at 12 noon, when I regained my senses; (like I had some to begin with) it was 2am the next day. That experience wasn't enough to keep me from smoking it again. The next time I went to Brooklyn to pick up some heroin. I took a cab to some God forsaken area and took care of my business and because I couldn't hail a cab on the street I decided to take

Poetic Recovery

the subway. I waited until I got in the train station and that is where I lit up a stick of Angel Dust. I got on the train at 3 o'clock in the morning and rode until 4 o'clock in the afternoon. Thank God for Arian because I did find my way to her house in Queens. That did it for me and I never smoked Angel Dust again.

I was 18 years old and I could go anywhere and work anywhere without question. I didn't have to think long about my next move. Where could I sell drugs and liquor and get paid for both? Voila, another afterhours spot!
There were several afterhours' spots in Harlem that I and my girlfriends had come to patronize during the 70's. There was the Hubba, Club 83, The Big Track (356) and Across the Tracks. These spots catered to the uptown hustlers who sold large quantities of dope primarily heroin and cocaine. They drank champagne and spent lots of money on their women. The primary commodity that enabled these hustlers to prosper was heroin. Hustlers were not nor have ever been limited to the male gender. Women gambled and sold drugs with the best of them. There was a family of females who contributed greatly to the distribution of cocaine, and heroin. They hailed from a bar known as the "The Dunbar." This bar was notorious for the best cocaine north of 125th street. I learned that unless you had a man who owned an afterhours spot the chances of getting hired as a barmaid were slim. That is unless you were willing to give

up some ass or sell drugs, or in most cases both. I didn't realize that my addiction was growing until I found myself traveling long distance for a better quality of cocaine. There was no crack then and I was limited to sniffing cocaine. On the days Jerry would lose big at the race track he would cut his cocaine to the point it became pure garbage. I for one would not sniff or sell any of it. It was then that I took to visiting the ladies of The Dunbar and buying weight. I would take it to work with me and sell it at the Pimps Palace. I would sell only to customers that I knew would never let on to Jerry that I was indeed cutting his throat. I learned through the years that selling garbage could ruin a reputation as a respected hustler and I hadn't been in the game long enough to risk losing a potential clientele. I made some very beneficial connections which provided a quality of cocaine that I had grown accustomed to. Doretta, Arian and I would make our rounds to Smalls Paradise, Mr.B's, The Shalimar and the Gold Lounge on Seventh Avenue for drinks from time to time. It was in these bars you could find any drug your palate desired in addition to being able to sell your own product, to only the people you knew. The manner in which everyone sold drugs would come to a screeching halt the moment Nicky Barnes was featured on the cover of the New York Times Sunday magazine.

Chapter Twenty Six

The one establishment that could provide the cash flow and the excitement I craved was "The Big Track" on Sugar Hill at 145th Street. Jerry and I would frequent this spot after we closed "The Pimp's Palace." The Big Track was open 24/7 and provided gambling for the heavy hitters, dope boys, drag boys, and stick-up kids. Anyone who was known to be getting big money was permitted to play in these games. The games most frequently played were Cee-Low / 4,5,6, and various card games such as skin, tonk Coon-Can and set back. Of course craps was a game that was always the prelude to the games the high rollers preferred. Craps enabled the high rollers to peep the amount of money other players were holding. It was New York Willie who whispered to me one night while I was tending bar in the Pimp's Palace that if and when I got tired of giving my money to pimps, he would welcome me into his spot where I would be on the receiving end of the cash flow as his woman. I managed to get hired and New York Willie was right. My first night working for him as a barmaid was quite impressive. As long as there was a game going on, there were tips flying into my pocket. For a brief moment I thought I wouldn't have to steal because the tips consisted of $20 and up. Now, to believe that I was actually New York Willie's woman was really a joke. He had a harem and they all acted as though they were actually the one and only ones. I dated him once, we went to the movies to see *Walking Tall*, the original version. We had dinner and sex and that was it. Our relationship was one of mutual admiration. I respected his ability to get money and he respected mine. I found him to be crude and barbaric in a ghetto sort of way. However, his money made him tolerable. During the week of my birthday I was angry with Rome, so I never gave him a medallion I had made for him. I allowed the jeweler to keep it until I could finish paying for this huge gold and diamond encrusted ram's head that hung on a heavy gold Gucci chain. I had three Aries men in my life and the only one making a respectable contribution to my favorite charity which-was- me, was New York Willie. The week of my 19th birthday New York Willie hit the street number for six figures. Though he was responsible for a lot of the cocaine and dope being sold in Harlem his first love was gambling. When he played he couldn't be disturbed. I witnessed on a couple of occasions the results of what happens to someone who interrupts him while he is gambling let's just say the victim always had to be carried out. In most cases a pistol upside the head and the nastiest cursing out anyone could imagine was his norm. I, wanting to defy tradition picked this time to present him with the gold medallion of the ram. It was my birthday and I was giving him a gift. He was so shocked at having been given

Poetic Recovery

anything from a woman he attempted to return it to me. Saying, "No woman has ever bought me anything so expensive." It was at that moment I knew I had made a good friend and secured my job for a little while longer. New York Willie was as generous as he was violent. It was this combination that caused him to be gunned down in broad daylight on Lenox Avenue in front of the Lenox Lounge; only to have the medallion snatched from his neck as his lifeless body lay bleeding on the sidewalk. The days that followed his death were filled with more bloodshed and violence. It was rumored that on a particular Sunday while I was turning a date with another dope boy Thunderball, a contract had been in play causing the deaths of two more respected hustlers by the name of Tink and Atlantic City Skeet. Their lifeless bodies were found stuffed in the trunk of a vehicle at Grant's Tomb on Riverside Drive. Things were getting hectic and the Big Track was becoming a place of interest to the police and more importantly the Feds. It was during this period that I met a gentleman named Lonnie Jenkins. He was a perfect gentleman at all times which is what attracted me to him. He was polite, well spoken and of course had plenty money. The fact that he was a high roller and never kept less than $50,000 in cash on him at all times was a huge plus. I knew with New York Willie out of the picture that my days were numbered working in the Big Track and Lonnie was just who I needed to lengthen my employment. New York Willie's partner, Herchel was an elderly, legally blind, wealthy man who loved cards and young girls. More importantly he and Lonnie were friends who exchanged money if needed. Lonnie was an older gentleman who was tall slender, light skinned, with salt and pepper hair. His eyes were light brown and they twinkled whenever he smiled. He was known for wearing Ivy League pullover sweaters, and signature matching caps. He knew of my reputation being a money maker who gave men jewelry on her birthday, and having a way with words. He also learned that I was struggling, to take a few college courses. He supported me fully, by giving me big tips whenever he gambled, and making sure that the other gamblers followed suit.

  After working my shift Lonnie would drop me off at my mother's house. I did not want any unnecessary drama since I continued to live with Rome in the projects. Lonnie had a connection with a florist and regularly sent me baskets of flowers that looked like funeral arrangements at least three times a week. If he was gambling he'd always put a few hundred dollars in my bra to take a cab. Oh, he too, had other women and a wife however; they never interfered with our relationship. I knew them and respected them whenever they would surface. He had no problem taking me out in public, and I had no problem letting him. We enjoyed late night dinners, concerts and major sporting events.

Poetic Recovery

When he was unable to escort me himself, he made sure I had a ticket and money to do with as I pleased. At least one night a week we ended up at the Skyline Motor Inn on 10th Avenue in Mid-Manhattan. Romance was Lonnie Jenkins specialty and I looked forward to our time together. I never knew if we were going to Las Vegas to a fight or to Pasadena for a Super Bowl. Lonnie was spontaneous with everything except parting with his money. When it came to money, every dollar was accounted for.

One piece of advice that Lonnie gave me was to always keep some money in the bank. It wasn't a priority at age nineteen and I didn't take heed. I believed at that age I would always have access to money, or better yet men with money. Lonnie had no problem with showing me how much he enjoyed me. On my 20th birthday I let him know how much I appreciated everything that he did for me, and presented him with a solid gold Dunhill lighter with his initials in diamonds. Unlike New York Willie, Lonnie was gracious when accepting my gift. His only remark was "It's good to know what good is!" Lonnie was not always readily available to me, and I often craved more excitement and attention than he could provide. He usually gambled with his friend Tex, who was also a high roller. Tex had many connections and business dealings from coast to coast. Tex was dating a young woman, Anita who originated from Detroit. She was married to a musician who was a drummer who was often on the road. She had two little girls and was often alone. A friend brought her to the Big Track where she met Tex. Her relationship was not unlike the one I had with Lonnie. She and I quickly became friends and went out together often on double dates with Lonnie and Tex. When there was a big game both Lonnie and Tex were guaranteed to be gambling until the wee hours of the morning. Anita and I would hang out together drinking, sniffing cocaine, and talking about men and money. Our common interest, was getting paid.

Chapter Twenty Seven

It was Anita who introduced me to her brother Mark. He had recently moved to New York from Detroit, and was by no means a square. He had just finished doing a ten year prison sentence for being involved in the shooting of a Detroit police officer. He was working in the field of computers and was struggling with trying to be a father and a tax paying citizen. This was a heavy task for someone who was use to getting money by means other than legal employment. When we first met I didn't entertain becoming involved with him on any level other than selling him cocaine. He was tall and sexy in a Scorpion kind of way. I didn't interpret his appearance as lethal at the time however time would tell another story. He purchased some cocaine from me the first night we met. This was the guise he used to acquire my phone number. After we exchanged numbers he pursued me day and night. I was intrigued by the magnitude of his interest in me. We began to see each other for dinner, lunch and any excuse I could think of just to be in his company. I began telling Lonnie lies just to be with Mark. I believed he genuinely enjoyed spending time with me. When I finally couldn't take anymore dates and small talk, I accepted an invitation to dinner at his apartment. Mark had a waterbed in a studio apartment on 152nd Street between Riverside Drive and Broadway. This location was convenient because it was near the Big Track where I still worked. Mark prepared what I like to call a *real man's meal*, steak, salad and baked potato. Mark had skills in more places than the kitchen. I assumed desert would be cocaine, boy was I wrong!

After the main course he poured me another glass of wine and fired up a joint of chunky black weed. He then led me from the kitchen table to the water bed. He removed my shoes, instructing me to relax. De Barge' was in the eight track player singing "I Call Your Name." Mark sat down beside me and began covering my face with tiny little kisses. Each one ignited a fuse that was preparing to explode. He undressed me slowly, then took my hand and led me to the shower. He was careful to make sure the water was tepid. He took his time and washed me gently, and allowed me to reciprocate. Every stroke of the cloth felt like tiny feathers fluttering over every nerve ending of my entire body. We rinsed and dried each other off, only to return to the warmth of the waterbed. What happened next was more than anything I anticipated or even imagined. It was more than I had dreamed of or had ever experienced in my life. All the corny stuff they talk about in movies and books took place that night. The earth moved, I saw fireworks, and I trembled to his every touch. We experimented with each other's bodies, finding each other's key spots where ecstasy to took over. The use of cocaine only served to heighten our pleasure. I knew from that moment a change was about to take place, in my soul, in my mind, in my heart and in my life.

    I continued to sell cocaine and work at the *Big Track.* When time permitted I would leave my job tending bar, jump in a cab and head for Mark's house during my lunch hour. I found myself wanting to do everything for this man. We talked constantly on the phone. I gave him the phone number to Rome's mother's house and my mother's house so he would always be able to contact me. It was because he was a man; he decided I should afford him the opportunity to go into the business of selling cocaine for himself. And so a partnership was formed that was destined to fail.

Life Don't Rhyme

WHAT DOES IT MEAN?

What does it mean when it comes to an old love?
There is no time limit on how long
memories will exist.
Long ago I believed my life to be bliss
When his name comes to mind I slip back in time
Remembering how it was when I believed
I was in love
Those beautiful melodic tunes,
That caused my heart to swoon
Whenever my love, would enter a room
Hearing those songs today make me crazy even now
Sparking a glimmer of hope that I may see him in a crowd.
After twenty years of hearing our favorite songs
I know exactly where we went wrong
The events that led us to part
Had been predestined to fail from the very start
I suffered from this great need to be loved
I fell hook, line, and sinker and time stood still
the moment he entered my life.
He made the courtship exquisite.
Met his family on a couple of visits
I disrespected myself and others too
Just to be able to hear someone say "I love you"
I manipulated people with each dawning of the sun
I truly believed I was in love with someone
Eventually the money was never enough

Poetic Recovery

With two using drugs, life got rough
So I began to star in a race
Just so I could see my lovers face
It was the mirror that informed me
I could withstand no more
He announced we had no future and walked
silently out the door,
Though it was long ago,
Twenty years later the memories are still sore
As I live and breathe today, I pray
The person I once was, has gone to stay
Because from where I sit, I am on my way
To live life sober and clean
It was not until I learned to love myself
That I understood what *I love you* means

Life Don't Rhyme

Chapter Twenty Eight

    I proceeded to pawn some of my jewelry in order to pay for two ounces of cocaine. I told Mark it was his responsibility to get back my initial investment of two thousand dollars. He could then capitalize off of his profit. All I wanted in return was my jewelry out of pawn. His plan was to take the cocaine to Detroit where his mother and sisters lived. He and I visited on a couple of occasions and there was definitely a demand for quality cocaine. Mark's younger sister Ya Ya had a growing clientele thanks to Anita who had been dealing for Tex since they first became involved. Mark had no problem doubling his profit. Mark was doing well with his new business venture and paid me back as previously agreed. Then the drama came. Mark called me at Rome's house and demanded I give him some money to leave New York. He knew I was still living in Rome's house and when I told him I couldn't give him any money he became enraged. He then said he was on his way over and I had better have some money or he would shoot everyone in the house. True to his word he came to the door with a 357 magnum under his coat. Rome wasn't at home but his mother was. I didn't want this woman to see this big gun in her home. I knew it wouldn't have taken a whole lot for her to be able to piece the situation together or worse come to her own conclusion. I could see in his eyes that he was on some crazy shit.

Poetic Recovery

He demanded the money in one breath and threatened to hurt someone in the next. In an effort to defuse the situation I managed to isolate him in the kitchen. I gave him the money I had on hand close to a thousand dollars. Mark took the money and ran out the door. Rome's mother was unaware that I knew him and I stuck to my story of it being a robbery. Ms.Vy called the police, and we made a report. Immediately following the robbery I moved into my mother's home. By then she had moved to the Bronx, 1600 Grand Concourse. She surely needed more room with my brothers and sisters living with her. I was in constant fear of Rome finding out what really happened in his home between Mark and me. My gut told me that Rome knew that I had something more to do with Mark's violating his home than I cared to admit. He never mentioned it and neither did I. The altercation with Mark was a close call, and though I was angry I was more hurt than anything else. What is even worse, I was ready to forgive him without giving a second thought as to what could have happened on the fateful day he threatened my life and the lives of the people I loved. I continued to keep in touch with his sister Anita. She explained to me that Mark had gotten into some trouble with the New York police which is why he came to Rome's house and took the money. He had to leave the state. I continued to work at the *Big Track* because it was one of the few ways I was able to keep tabs on where Mark was and how he was doing. His sister wouldn't give me his exact whereabouts however she would relay my messages to him. He would call me from time to time and tell me he regretted what he had done and how he acted. He went on to further explain that he was not returning to New York because of a warrant that had been issued for his arrest. He continued to tell me that he loved and missed me terribly but would never risk his freedom by returning to New York.

      Lonnie and I continued to see each other however our affair fizzled having been informed by Tex that I had been involved with Mark. Lonnie and I still remained friends throughout the years. He would rescue me many times in my life and for his friendship I am truly grateful. I soon stopped working at the *Big Track* and just sold cocaine and dope as I needed in order keep money in my pocket. I also continued to give my mother money to pay bills and take care of my siblings. Rome was useful in that area. He always managed to keep a clientele to help me get rid of dope as quickly has I got hold to it. Rome was no longer given heroin to sell on consignment due to his addiction to Angel Dust. No one could risk his passing out and waking up without his work. We remained friends through every episode of my life. There is not much you can do to help someone else when you are twisted yourself. Not knowing who you are or much less where you are going could only prove disastrous. I learned that in order for a relationship to grow, the people involved must be honest with themselves and each other. The willingness to sacrifice in an effort to grow together had not taken priority in my life during this time. Many years would pass before I would be faced with making a decision that would require sacrifice in order to save my own life. What's more important is that I not try to recreate others into what I want them to be. All I can do is meet them where they are.

Life Don't Rhyme

Chapter Twenty Nine

During the spring of 1978, despite the drama I created in my life, I became quite preoccupied with my appearance. I don't know if it was because I robbed Tex of an enormous amount of cocaine or because I robbed one of Lonnie's gambling partners, Jimmy Halston of a great deal of money in Las Vegas. (Who the hell hides money under a mattress in Vegas?) For numerous reasons I began looking for new hair styles and a stylist who would provide me with a special look, that would scream independent female hustler who was not to be fucked with. I had recently attended a fashion show where I met a model whose hair style caught my eye. I inquired as to where she had gotten it done and who her stylist was. She graciously provided me with the information and I made an appointment the same week . The fact that the salon was downtown on the lower West Side of 23rd Street told me one important thing the patrons had money. In my mind in order to make money one must surround one's self with those people with money.

It was a quaint salon called Hairobi's a complete day spa. It was equipped to cater to every cosmetic need, facials, nails, pedicures, manicures, waxing, sauna's, and massage. It was elegant, efficient and Black owned. It was exactly the type of establishment I was looking for since I was beginning to increase my very

Poetic Recovery

busy drug business. Hairobi's provided me with a location outside of Harlem where I could attend to all my personal needs at one time in addition to making some extra money. I didn't have to worry about someone coming to buy cocaine, or dope from me while I was under the dryer, unlike Ace's Barbershop on Eighth Avenue and 146th street. Also it would reduced my chances of leaving the salon looking like a clone. I became a loyal patron of Hairobi's and quickly became friends with the owner, Lorna. We often had time to chit -chat over wine and champagne. I always had cocaine and a few of her stylists indulged so that was a plus because with stylists as narcotic consumers came more customers. Along with Hairobi's customers came exciting, elegant, high profile events where people powdered their noses and I was always invited; however my first priority was to be discreet at all costs.

    One afternoon during a facial I informed Lorna that I was single and in the market for a man with whom I could be myself. She let me know that her husband Angel had a brother, Nicky, who was single, working and had also been recently released from prison. She arranged a phone call between Nicky and I during my next appointment. I began feeling him out over the phone for an entire week. We talked daily until, I felt comfortable enough to set up a date. Nicky was twenty-five years my senior and a little on the short side for my taste, but a very nice guy all the same. I remained focused on what an asset he could become should the relationship take off. We met for dinner, he was well dressed in dapper sort of way. What stood out was that he still managed to exude a hustler's spirit. I could sense that he was somewhat intimidated by my youth and independence, yet this did not deter his interest in me. I remained guarded during our first date. He on the other hand was open and honest about himself and his past. I soon found out that he, too, was needy. He confided in me that he was on Parole and also an ex-dope addict. How could his brother be married to my hair stylist Lorna? Well he was, and his name was Angel. Angel, had a considerable amount of power and money in the current drug game throughout New York State. The problem was Nicky having been an active addict had done some very despicable things concerning drug transactions that never showed a profit. These schemes caused Nicky's brother to cut him off from having anything to do with "the business." That was all the information I needed to hear. I gradually enlightened Nicky about my current career, and what my immediate goals were. We began to date and more times than not I usually stood him up because I was working or just didn't want to be bothered. When I did see him, he always questioned me about what happened or where I was. This was a true sign that Nicky was falling in love with me. He tolerated far too much disrespect from me. I'll give him credit for figuring out that the only way to keep tabs on what he believed to be his pussy was to provide the commodity that kept me employed, heroin. I was still in the mindset that if I was giving up "*my body*" I would never pay for any dope. However, I had to rethink the situation like a business woman who anticipated a long and profitable relationship, with my potential brother n law. Nicky offered to get me some dope that was a better quality than the dope I was currently selling. I immediately accepted this invitation as a sign that he was ready to approach his brother about our relationship. Nicky informed me that it would be my product. This meant that I could continue working when I pleased. The catch was that I would relocate from Harlem to Queens and hustle from a bar on Liberty Avenue, "*The Black Kat Lounge.*" It was a business deal that became more appealing than I dared to dream. As time passed I was flipping my packages between Harlem and Queens so fast that I developed a genuine business relationship with Nicky's brother Angel. He provided me with as much dope as I could sell. My responsibility was to make sure that Nicky never used heroin again. Angel figured that since I was his brother's woman, I was also his brother's keeper. Nicky and I developed a very profitable arrangement. I explained to Nicky I would conduct my business the way I saw fit and did not require a baby sitter. I put together my own crew and rarely sold heroin hand to hand unless I chose to, however, Nicky had other ideas. He called me all day long he constantly questioned my whereabouts and who I was with. It dawned on me that Nicky thought I was his wife, which worked because I thought I had the French Connection.

    I moved in with Nicky and played house as often as I needed to refresh my package. Life was great. I no longer had to pay for grooming at Hairobi's other than tips for the help. Often cash tips were replaced with either dope or cocaine. Business was great at Hairobi's for Lorna as well. This woman had skills and a way with the public that made anyone who entered her establishment want to spend all of their money. Her business savvy allowed her to open a second salon Hairobi's II in Forest Hills in addition to an elegant boutique on Seventh Avenue around the corner from the first shop.

Chapter Thirty

I knew my cash flow would stop if I didn't secure my position in Nicky's life. So I decided we should marry. I had become acquainted with some hustlers who were based in Queens while working at the "*Big Track*" in Harlem. These gentlemen had no problem in taking work from me once they realized the dope was good and plentiful. I spoke to Nicky's brother Angel about getting more weight. All that was needed was my assurance that I would have no problem moving the dope. More importantly that he would be paid, and, of course, that I continue to make sure his brother Nicky never came in contact with it. I began making frequent trips to Rochester where I often doubled my money, and in most cases, quadrupled it. I put together a crew in Queens to manage the dope sales at the *Black Kat* bar. I occasionally hit my girlfriend Doretta off with a little something because her man Jamar had caught a case and was doing a bid. Doretta and I always had an unspoken arrangement, that whoever had a man with drugs would look out for the other; which meant we always paid ourselves first. I still had an ongoing relationship with my childhood friend Lettie who still lived and worked in Rochester. Lettie's Uncle Juni, and I established a business arrangement that allowed everyone involved to be paid handsomely. When I saw that the money seemed to be endless I spread the love to Rome.

Life Don't Rhyme

I gave him enough dope to keep some money in his pocket and take care of his mother and nephews. He was my friend and I never wanted to see him go without. Though he always came up short he did have the majority of my money when time came to replenish his supply. The time to introduce Nicky to my mother arrived, and when I did she was not impressed in the least. She knew I had an ulterior motive for dating this old man. I gave my mother some money and of course she was as gracious as she was suspicious. My brothers and sisters knew I had found another Sugar Daddy. They also knew their sister had one purpose in mind, to ride off into the sunset and live happily ever after with Mark.

I proposed to Nicky in room 222 of the Kew Motor Lodge on the Union Turnpike in Queens. He accepted my proposal and my fairytale wedding began to unfold. We informed Nicky's brother Angel and his wife Lorna of the upcoming nuptials. Angel appeared to be happy for his brother, so much so he gave me two ounces of China White heroin which could be cut forty times. He informed me that this gift was to pay for the wedding of my dreams. I got the word out about the quality of the dope I was selling, and the money began coming in rapidly. Everything was going exactly as I had anticipated. I was accepted into the business and the family and Angel and I continued to do great business. I witnessed firsthand how treacherous the drug trade is, and could be while working at the Big Track. I always kept up front that Angel was deadly, ruthless, and charming all rolled up into one handsome Portuguese man with a temper. The future of my business greatly depended on how tight lipped my business associates remained. Nicky and I became closer, and he began to reveal just how needy he was. I wouldn't find out to what extent until after the wedding. I had successfully managed to start the wheels rolling toward becoming a part of a family that could either get me killed or make me rich. I wasn't taking any chances, I had a plan and it began by saying the words I do.

In the 1978 June issue of *Essence* Magazine, I found a layout for summer weddings. The beauty of the designs and the wardrobe of the bridal parties caught my eye. I contacted the magazine and gathered the information of where I could find the same fabric used in the magazine layout. Nicky and I, his brother Angel and Lorna went out to dinner to discuss our future. We set a date and made plans for a late summer wedding. It was guaranteed to be one of my finest performances.

Life Don't Rhyme

I DO

Well I'm all grown up, believe me it was rough
I finally escaped, to keep from being raped.
Went to high school by day, sold dope by night
Moved to the deluxe apartment in the sky
Managed an afterhours spot, traveled overseas
Every day I counted G's.
I'd graduated high school by then
It's safe to say I had been around the block and back again
That way of life became a bore
I knew in my life there had to be more
So I opened the 1978 bridal issue of *Essence* Magazine
And there it was the wedding of my dreams
It did not matter whether or not I was in love.
To pay for this wedding I had to sell drugs
I proceeded to my favorite beauty salon,
Where I found, my aging drug dealing Don Juan
He didn't hesitate for one second
He immediately said *yes* when I popped the question.
To pay for this wedding I sold two ounces of pure dope
And because good dope will make a dope fiend greedy
On my wedding day two people overdosed
The wedding was spectacular
It went off without a hitch.
Two days later my new husband I ditched
You see I was 23 and he was 56,
What I wanted was the wedding.
Not the husband that went with it.

Poetic Recovery

Chapter Thirty One

My pre-wedding gift from my brother in law Angel gave me access to a cash flow I believed would last forever. My girlfriend Lettie remained my friend and kept in touch with me from the moment I moved to New York. I contacted her and announced my plans to be married. I designated Lettie as my maid of honor. As for overseeing the dope business in Rochester, she became my right hand while I attended to the wedding plans in New York. I made enough money to cover all expenses and still managed to have more dope I hadn't been prepared for sale. My soon to be sister in law Lorna came up with a great idea to celebrate her wedding anniversary in Las Vegas, Nevada. She invited a few choice customers to accompany her and her husband Angel. It was perfect because *Larry Holmes* and *Ken Norton* were fighting at *Caesar's Palace* on June 9th. I loved boxing and it was a perfect event to make more money. It was also the perfect time to revisit my feelings for Mark. It was at that moment I called Mark's sister Anita and told her about my plans to marry. I begged her to contact Mark before I went through with this joke of a marriage. She didn't let me down. Twenty four hours later I was on the phone with Mark, and we agreed to meet each other in Las Vegas. He was living and working in Los Angeles, which was less than an hour's flight to Las Vegas.

Life Don't Rhyme

My future in-laws and I flew out of LaGuardia Airport, and before the flight took off I had sold an ounce of cocaine on the plane. Upon my arrival in Las Vegas I immediately sent Mark a round trip ticket from Los Angeles to Las Vegas, Nevada. My in-laws spared no expense and reserved a beautiful suite for me. I had no interest in any of the activities going on in the hotel. My primary focus was seeing Mark. I utilized a limousine, compliments of the MGM Grand Hotel and met Mark at the airport. The sight of his 6'3" frame caused me to become weak at the knees, tremble, and shake uncontrollably. I was overwhelmed with emotion. As the tears poured from my eyes, he lifted my face and kissed the tears as they fell. He dropped his bag to the floor and allowed his mouth to travel down my face, and rest on my lips and began what seemed to be the longest kiss on earth. Passionately his mouth devoured mine as we tasted each other. My body still trembling was surrounded by his strong arms, letting me know the past was in the past, and that I was safe. We rode back to the hotel and locked ourselves in my suite for close to thirty-six hours. We made passionate love like teenagers who were trying to recapture some hidden treasure that could only be found together. We ate, drank and sniffed cocaine. We enjoyed the Jacuzzi in the room that afforded us yet another venue for love making. I told Mark of my plan to get married and leave my husband

Poetic Recovery

immediately following the wedding reception with all the gifts, drugs and cash. I told him that I still loved him and could not imagine being without him any longer. *(Talk about youth being wasted on the young)* It was then, he asked if I would move to Los Angeles with him and of course my answer was yes. When we did emerge from my hotel suite in the *MGM Grand* hotel I introduced Mark to my in-laws as an old friend who had come to Las Vegas on business. Oddly enough no one not my brother in law Angel or his wife, Lorna questioned me as to where I had been the past thirty-six hours. Of course I didn't volunteer any information. All one had to do was take one look at me to know that something was definitely up. When time came for Mark to return to Los Angeles, I gave him enough money to buy a car, so that he could have transportation to pick me up when I arrived at LAX airport. The wedding was set for
September 3rd and I had reservations to leave for Los Angeles the morning of September 4th.

     When I returned from Las Vegas I put everything in motion in preparation for my wedding. I ordered five hundred gold engraved invitations, a Rolls Royce limousine, ice sculptures, gardenias and had the bridesmaids fitted for their saris. My dress was being sewn according to the specifications of the magazine's design. Nicky was fitted for his suit, as was the best man. Everything was exactly as shown in the magazine. I rented the hall for the reception

Life Don't Rhyme

and planned the menu for the wedding dinner as well. I hired my old boyfriend King the art teacher to take the wedding pictures. King had made a name for himself as an artist and photographer, and I couldn't think of anyone I would rather have make that money. Everything was set to go except the minister to perform the ceremony. It was common knowledge that all weddings performed by Nana were destined to fail, so it seemed only fitting that she perform my ceremony. More importantly I would not be required to pay her. She graciously provided the space for the ceremony itself. Nana's home has always been a show place that sits on a tree lined street with a front yard that practically spans the block. The front yard is trimmed with four rows of flowers that extend from the front of the house to the back. I enlisted the services of a landscaper and instructed him to erect a white Gazebo on the front lawn, in front of a flower bed that was filled with roses, pansies, and daffodils all in full bloom. Daddy Bob would play the piano, and as planned Lettie, was my maid of honor. Lettie's Uncle Juni gave me away because my father refused. He knew I was up to no good. Daddy always knew when I was up to something. My father was more aware of my true intentions than I was. He refused to be a part of my charade. Strange, how he just picked up on the fact that I intended to ditch my new husband. He had met Mark only once when I took him to Rochester. I was shocked because Daddy

Poetic Recovery

allowed us to sleep in the same room in the home he shared with his wife Liz. My father being the gracious host that he is, entertained Mark and treated him like I had never witnessed him treat any male friend of *mine* before in my life. It was during this visit that I believe he recognized my feelings for Mark were serious.

On the morning of the ceremony, Daddy Bob's aunt was found dead on the toilet, located on the first floor of Nana's house where I was scheduled to be married in less than four hours. Then one of my workers informed me the police were also investigating the death of an overdose victim who was believed to have consumed the heroin that was in circulation. I was consumed with my plans and gave none of the tragedies a second thought. I was getting married and that was all I was concerned with.

All in all it was a beautiful ceremony and I received countless gifts and four thousand dollars in cash. My maid of honor and I disappeared after the reception. I called my new husband on the phone and instructed him to return to the hotel where I would meet him later. Well, later was the next day at check out time. Lettie and I took the limo and hung out all night in Rochester getting high with the limo driver, who was a cutie pie. My husband and I never consummated the marriage nor did I offer an explanation as to why I was missing on our wedding night. I simply told him that I would be in touch, and that I had some unfinished

Life Don't Rhyme

business to attend to in California. With that being said he sat down on the edge of the bed in the hotel room and watched as I gathered all the gifts and money and walked out the door. Lettie drove me to the airport where I boarded my non-stop flight to Los Angeles LAX airport.

    Time has prevented me from making amends to many of the people my active addiction harmed. I deeply apologize and ask for forgiveness. I believed for so many years the things I did took no toll on anyone other than myself. I was wrong. A snowball affect took place in my life, and to this day I am not quite sure when it began. I do know that the avalanche came close to being fatal. It was while I was on these slopes of death that I called for the help of a power greater than myself, God.

Chapter Thirty Two

Mark met me just as planned. He picked me up in a red two door Honda Civic which he purchased with the money I had given him in Las Vegas. I was feeling good, and hopeful that our life together was finally going to be what I imagined. We drove to what was now our apartment located on Harvard and Fifth Street near Western Boulevard. We dropped off the luggage where I had stashed the cocaine and dope I brought with me. I informed Mark that since I wasn't familiar with LAPD and their tactics, I didn't think it would be wise to ride around Los Angeles with narcotics in the car. He agreed the drugs would be safer in the apartment. I was excited, hungry and suffering from jet lag, and far from being ready to go to sleep. We started with lunch at Fat Burgers, and then proceeded to do a little sightseeing in Beverly Hills and Malibu. The perfect ending to a perfect day ended in each other's arms soaking wet from making love that can only be described as delicious. Back then you could never have made me believe that sex was an addiction. Little did I know I was deeply confused and suffering from low self-esteem. The hard hearted person that had prevailed in New York was about to come face to face with a new monster that would require everything I had to give. This monster's name was" Free Base," better known as Crack!

Life Don't Rhyme

Our studio apartment was sparsely furnished, with the necessities an eight track player, a bed, a couch and a television. It was barely big enough for the two of us; however love turned it into a mansion. The apartment building was populated with very colorful people. Most of whom engaged in illegal activities. Mark and I agreed I would continue to sell cocaine to his clientele and that he would continue to work. I had relatives who lived in the Laurel Canyon area and I knew they would be an asset for drumming up business. Mark told me about a new form of cocaine on the rise and there seemed to be a high demand for it in the Los Angeles area. He told me it was called Free Base. The recipe was not considered illegal because the word cocaine had been omitted from the recipe. You could purchase your *Free Base* kit in your local grocery store. One evening, Mark gave me a demonstration. I gave him some cocaine and he placed a gram in a clear shaker bottle, combined with ether. He shook it in the shaker bottle until a white mixture coated the sides of the bottle. Then, with a torch he heated the bottle until the white coating melted from the sides and rested in the bottom of the bottle. In the bottom of the bottle lay what appeared to be a yellow bubble. Carefully he unscrewed the top and placed the bottle to my nose. The fumes smelled exactly like the inside of a hospital. He then dipped the bottle into a bowl of ice water swirling it around and around, until I heard a clinking sound. What he showed me was a hardened rock. He explained to me it was the yellow bubble I had seen earlier in the bottom of the bottle which had hardened. He explained that in this form it was now in its purest state and ready to be smoked. He extracted the rock from the bottle and placed it on a plate. With a razor blade he shaved the rock back into powder. He offered me what looked to be a water pipe filled with the white snowflake looking crystals. He lit a Q-tip that had been dipped in over proof rum. As he melted the cocaine on the pipe he then instructed me to inhale.

After all that preparation, I didn't feel a damn thing. An entire month would pass before I began to enjoy smoking "*Free Base*". With Mark at work and me alone in the apartment I had plenty of time to practice. I was still focused on making money. However, smoking cocaine didn't thrill me yet so I continued to sniff the cocaine as I always had. I continued to take trips back and forth to New York to replenish my supply of cocaine and to check on my mother, brothers, and sisters. It was always during these brief visits that my mother would inform me that my husband Nicky was frantic with worry and was looking all over for me. It was even rumored that he may have resumed using heroin. Upon finding out this information I decided to contact him. I anticipated Nicky would use my leaving him as an excuse to use heroin. While talking to him over the phone, what I learned was that he assumed I would apologize for leaving him. I zinformed him that I was not a stay at home wife and that our marriage would never have worked out. I also informed him that I was not taking any of the blame for his returning back to his beloved heroin. That was the last time I spoke to Nicky.

    Meanwhile in Los Angeles, Mark had utilized my absence to import a wanna be actress girlfriend, Neva from New York to visit him in Los Angeles. I discovered she was in town when he was late to pick me up from the airport. I was livid having arrived with more than two ounces of cocaine on me, coming through the security gate at the airport. When I saw him I gave him the baggage checks so that he could retrieve my luggage. Since he was late I wanted him to sweat and feel what it was like wondering if you were going to be singled out for a random search. I was more than sure that he would have no problem. He didn't, and met me outside with my bags in hand. He kissed me and began to apologize for being late. He led the way to the car in the parking lot. As I approached the car I saw two sets of skis on top of the hood of the car I bought. I asked "Who were you skiing with?" He replied "Neva." I recalled her being one of his old flames from New York who had hopes of becoming an actress. I was angry and asked him why on earth could he not just bring her to the airport with him rather than place me at risk by picking me up late? He responded with "she is not as open minded as you." It occurred to me to

Poetic Recovery

ask him where she was staying during her visit. When he told me a hotel I went ballistic. I said "if she loves you like I love you then she can come and stay with us and save that cash; after all she is sniffing our cocaine!" It was at that moment I realized I had given Mark the confirmation he needed to know that he could do anything he wanted, and I would still be there with him and for him. Soon after this incident I began smoking cocaine more often. Business was often slow in the day so I had plenty of time to teach myself how to prepare and smoke free base. What I learned was that Mark had not taught me all there was to know about cooking and smoking cocaine. Greed reared its ugly head into our relationship and deceit and mistrust quickly followed. I recall taking a bust for forgery and doing some time in Sybil Brand Correctional Facility for Women in Los Angeles while we were together. Not one time did Mark come to see me. I still remained with this man refusing to believe that he had no love or respect for me. As time continued he began taking more trips back east and of course smoking more cocaine. I continued to commit forgery and turn tricks all the while believing I was securing my position as Mark's woman. One weekend as Mark was preparing to leave and visit his family in Detroit, I got it into my head that he was cheating and not telling me with whom. I had always known Mark was a whore and graciously accepted that indiscretion in our relationship. As long as I knew who it was, I never allowed it to become a major concern. However this time I had no clue and was angry as hell. I refused to question him about it because I didn't want to appear as though I was insecure or jealous. What was worse I had begun to play around with the thought that I may just be addicted to Mark. I had recently begun learning how to drive a stick shift and had gotten my permit. The morning Mark was to leave for Detroit, I packed his suitcase and he informed me that he was driving the car to the airport and leaving it parked there until he returned. Since I had a set of keys, I decided to go get the car myself and use it while he was gone. I picked up the car around eleven o'clock on a Friday night. I paid for the parking and drove onto the Santa Monica freeway with no problem. I went to some bars and a couple of afterhour's spots in the Crenshaw district where I was able to sell some cocaine. I stayed out until 6 o'clock in the morning. I decided to get some gas before I called it a night. The station was a block away from the apartment, so I filled up the tank, paid for the gas. As I was preparing to leave the pump I put the car in the wrong gear and drove straight through the plate glass window of the 711 store. I was high, frantic, and didn't have a clue as to what to do. I went into the store and explained my situation, to the owner. I paid him eight hundred dollars for his windows and he allowed me to leave without making a police report. What I needed was to get

Poetic Recovery

the car repaired right away. Well, it was the weekend and that proved to be impossible. Mark came home and was furious. He was so mad he told me I had to move. He later explained to me he had not paid the insurance on the car, and it was best that I learn how to live on my own in Los Angeles without him. My first thought was to attempt suicide, in hopes that Mark would reconsider his decision to discontinue our relationship. I quickly threw that idea out the window because even though I loved him, I loved me more. He agreed to give me some time, to accumulate enough money for the move. The truth is, I was addicted to Mark and his incredible love making. I was angry with myself for being stupid enough to think I meant more to him than the car, or his ski trips with his wanna be actress. I learned you can't do dirt to others without getting some dirt thrown back in your own face.

Life Don't Rhyme

Chapter Thirty Three

    I was not without resources, and had initiated a relationship with one of my neighbors who worked as a dominatrix in an S and M / B and D brothel. She recommended me for a job there, and I was hired as a submissive. I was paid nicely for allowing some of the patrons to spank me and perform other devilish acts of degradation upon my body. Because I am not into pain, I quickly rose through the ranks to become a Dominatrix. I found that I enjoyed being on the other side much more because I got to administer the pain. I kept in touch with Mark because he was a good customer when it came to buying my cocaine.
    You see it was my cocaine now, and not ours. I made the transition to a single independent addict very quickly. He would rather purchase his cocaine from me, knowing that he could get a little something extra if he brought me a sale for someone other than himself. In addition to being the best lover I had ever experienced in my life, he could be counted on to come to my rescue as long as it didn't put his freedom at risk. Another important perk was that Mark still wanted to make love to me and he knew I would never pass up an opportunity.
    Thanks to my till tapping (cash register robbery) friend Marlow from Chicago I saved up enough money and moved into a very nice apartment on Vista Street off of Sunset

Poetic Recovery

Boulevard. It was a one bedroom apartment and served as a great location for my cocaine business. Free Base was alive and well and controlling every aspect of my life. The brothel where I worked was rumored to be owned by Larry Flint the creator of Hustler Magazine. His name alone made for an incredible clientele. The managers were strict about the girls not getting high so I didn't solicit any of my co-workers or customers for my business. I worked for several months before discovering my ticket out, or so I thought. I was already keeping company with a gentleman I knew little about, however he served as a physical replacement for Mark and enjoyed getting high.

    One morning very early while at work, a customer came in and explained he was relocating his business to Los Angeles from Baltimore. He informed the manager that he wanted a session on the premises, in addition to taking one of the girls with him to his hotel until the banks opened at 9 o'clock that morning. All the girls lined up, in hopes of being selected. The customer began pulling out stacks of one hundred dollar bills and an assortment of fine jewelry all of which he was carrying in a briefcase. He threw a stack of one hundred dollar bills to me on the couch where I was sitting. The bills were still new, complete with the bank wrapper. Then he asked "Have you ever seen that much money sweetie?" I

Life Don't Rhyme

answered, "no and that's not real money what do you think I'm, a sucker?" I knew it was real the moment I caught it in my hand. He made his selection from the girls and took his girl to one of the private rooms. I walked quickly to the nearest outside pay phone and called Mark. I instructed him to get me a wig, a trench coat, and a car that could be reported stolen after we accomplished our mission. I was aware that this Vic and my co-worker would be leaving at the end of the two hour session he had paid for. When Mark arrived I announced I was going to get something to eat. As the customer pulled out of the parking lot we pulled out behind him being careful not to bring any attention to ourselves. It wasn't until the customer exited on to the Santa Monica Freeway that Mark signaled to get in front of the Vic's car. When the time was right, Mark stopped short causing the Vic to bang into the back of our car. I jumped out of the car and proceeded to walk over to the passenger's side of the Vic's car. My co-worker didn't have a clue as to who I was, or for that matter what was about to happen. The customer, still seated behind the wheel of his car began shouting that it was his fault and he didn't want any problems and would be happy to pay for any damages. Mark was carrying a gun and slapped the Vic upside head, told him to shut up and took the keys out of the ignition. Mark threw me the keys and I opened the trunk and removed the briefcase I had seen earlier. Mark retrieved the

Poetic Recovery

Vic's wallet and all the remaining jewelry he was wearing. My co-worker sat there dumfounded and crying. I took the keys and threw them over the guard rail into the brush. We got back into our car and drove away. We ditched the car, wiped it down for fingerprints and reported it stolen. We split one hundred and fifty thousand dollars in cash and another hundred thousand dollars in jewelry. We checked into the Hilton Hotel where I placed my money and jewelry in the hotel safe. I didn't trust Mark and that was the bottom line. We shared a cab and he dropped me off at work. An hour later my co-worker came back to tell us what happened. I pretended to be very shocked, and inquired whether or not she was alright and more importantly if she could describe the thieves. She replied no! Two hours later the
detectives arrived to ask questions concerning the robbery. They were non-caring and stated that they had no sympathy for the Vic. They also said he was to blame, for not having gone to the bank first, before coming to get his ass spanked. After finishing my shift I met Mark at the hotel where we made love for what would be the last time. I knew I could never be with him again. One year later I met Mark in New York and summoned all my remaining strength to inform him that I loved him, but didn't need him. His response was a kiss and complete silence as he walked into the subway.

Life Don't Rhyme

See Ya

I cannot love you, if loving you means
I will lose myself
I have come to realize, I too need help
I cannot help you
Until I help myself
I cannot kiss it
And make it better for you
For you see I am wounded too.
When you fall
I can no longer pick you up
For if I do, your love may leave me stuck
There is nothing you can say
I wish to hear
My inner voice whispers softly
Have no fear
I will no longer beg you to stay with me
For it is not with me that you should be.
I am taking all that I am
And all I shall become
To ensure my life as a strong woman
A woman capable of loving herself first
Before ever attempting to love someone else

Poetic Recovery

The next morning I took the money and moved into another apartment. I sent my mother some money, bought some groceries, and a couple of pieces of furniture and a round trip airline ticket for New York. My current lover and I began getting high for what may have been five days. I fell asleep with a large portion of money in my boot. When I regained consciousness, the money was gone and I had been robbed!

    The old cliché "What goes around comes around" literally revealed itself to me. This payback let me know God didn't like ugly. The one thing I bought that was still in my possession was an airline ticket back to New York. I gathered up the few pieces of jewelry I had stashed, my small wardrobe and whatever else I could fit into my suitcase, tucked my tail between my legs and flew home, back to New York.

Life Don't Rhyme

Chapter Thirty Four

Upon my arrival in New York I returned to my mother's house. I explained to her that I was going to get a job, however I needed some time to find one. She was all for that. What she was not aware of was that I had returned with a habit that had become my job, full time.

I looked up my friend Doretta who I kept in touch with during my stay in Los Angeles. During that time Doretta and her man Jamar had also become acquainted with Free Base. In my absence Doretta had given birth to a baby boy, Jamar II. She also moved from her mother's home into her own apartment with Jamar in Lenox Terrace with their new baby boy. I spoke to Doretta frequently while living in Los Angeles. During these phone calls she informed me that Free Base was on the rise in New York. She eventually asked me for the recipe for how to cook cocaine. Apparently when Jamar was preparing the cocaine, it didn't always come out correctly. I instructed Doretta to save all the cocaine solution that Jamar thought he had messed up until I returned to New York. When I arrived at her house she pulled out glass jars from under the sink, the closet and anywhere she could store it. I knew every jar contained Free Base that Jamar deemed unsalvageable. I also knew that it could indeed be brought back to its purest form, by me. I considered myself a master at salvaging what was believed to have

Poetic Recovery

been lost. I thought for a minute about how I had become so lost yet unwilling to save myself. Unlike cocaine that only needed some simple preparation to restore it back to its purest form I would require more to be restored. I was amazed at how many containers of cocaine solution Doretta had saved. That afternoon I went to work and managed to salvage close to fourteen grams of cocaine that Jamar thought was lost. I went so far as to open up the pipes under the sink in the kitchen and the bathroom where he had poured much of the cocaine solution down the drains. Sure enough it had crystallized on the pipes. I went to work and brought back a piece of crack the size of a 33 inch record. Back then it was called a cookie because of its shape. Doretta and I made a profit, however a lot of it we just smoked ourselves. Soon after this Doretta confided in me that she and Jamar had really gone overboard with smoking free base. She explained that she was going to have to move back into St. Nicholas Projects with her mother and children. Doretta was strong then and remains a strong, loyal friend to this day.
She did whatever was necessary to ensure the safety and the well being of her children, family and friends. Doretta gave birth to another baby girl, Zekia. Doretta's man Jamar was always a good provider, however once he divorced smoking Free Base he gave new meaning to the word hustler. Getting money was his favorite past time; with the exception of taking his son

Life Don't Rhyme

Jamar II to see the Yankees play. Doretta and I still had a few more learning experiences to go through before we would stop the madness that accompanies the job of smoking cocaine. Then presto, just like that Doretta ended her abuse of the drug. Soon after this blessing took place Jamar Sr was a victim of a senseless killing that left everyone who loved him devastated.

    Still needing a job I found out that my previous employer from the *Pimp's Palace* Jerry, had relocated uptown and opened up another after hours spot on Seventh Avenue, between Chicken Man and the Shalimar. Needing a job I went to see him and he put me to work as a barmaid. Jerry's wife Blondine had become a visible fixture in this spot unlike at the Pimp's Palace, where she only surfaced to stir up some shit among Jerry's other women. I knew working for Jerry was not going to be as beneficial as it had once been in the *Pimp's Palace*. Blondine was watching every dollar that came across the bar. However, where there is a will, there is a way especially for a crack head. It was my job to find a way, because if there was nothing else I was willing to do on this earth, I was willing to get money to feed an addiction that had left my life unmanageable. Of course my cunning baffling and insidious. disease allowed me to believe I was in control insane uh?

Poetic Recovery

Chapter Thirty Five

Seventh Avenue had always been the main strip in Harlem. It was filled with hustlers dope boys, drag boys and of course pimps. At night all these characters came out for business dealings, fun, and games. The Gold Lounge, Small's Paradise, the Shalimar and Mr. B's served as the back drop for many transactions. If you were hungry there were several places where you could satisfy your palate sitting down or standing up. There was Adell's run by my friend Geraldine and her husband Homie, Sylvia's, Well's House of Chicken and Waffles, the Jap and my favorite Chicken Man. I learned Jerry's spot also doubled as a place for customers to smoke Free Base, which was known in New York City as crack. I had been smoking cocaine for three years before it exploded onto the New York scene. I was one of a handful of people who knew how to cook it three different ways. I offered my skills out for hire and was able to get high for free and keep money in my pocket for awhile. But like any drug, the tell tale signs of use appeared and I began stealing to feed my habit. This caused me to fall from grace with the circle of people who were the shakers and movers of the drug game. Jerry finally could no longer take the loss of the money I was stealing from him nightly as a barmaid and ultimately fired me. Jerry was a good man, his wife Blondine however, was a greedy, grimy selfish bitch who put her own husband in the line of fire. He was killed the same night he fired me by an unknown assailant so the story goes. Although there was a lot of speculation as to who would benefit from his death, no one was ever formally charged. It became very clear that I needed another hustle and I needed it fast. Doretta introduced me to an acquaintance, Narie. She was a local girl who lived in Doretta's building in St. Nicholas Projects. Now Narie's current boyfriend was in need of some females to accompany him and a friend on a trip to the Bahamas. The purpose of this trip was to return with two key loads of cocaine. We were being paid virtually nothing which I didn't come to find out until it was too late. The trip and the accommodations though plush, did not make up for the money I knew I should have been paid for taking such a risk. Through my ability to find out what was happening on Paradise Island I found the local establishment that catered to guest who smoked Free Base. One night I visited and spent a few hours there doing my thing. The moment I ran out of cocaine, I returned back to the hotel undetected. That same morning I appeared to have inhaled courage, in addition to the fumes of cocaine during my brief playtime. It was that courage and my greed that caused the entire venture to go down the toilet. That afternoon while window shopping, Narie and I stumbled upon a shop that sold exquisite sequin dresses. I helped myself to one of those dresses and returned to the hotel where the cocaine was being prepared for its return to New York. What I didn't know was that the police had followed Narie and I back to the hotel. They burst through the door of the room and took us to jail along with our two male companions. They only detained Narie's man and his partner. They confiscated the dress, all the cocaine, and everyone's luggage.

    The men were allowed to go free and return to New York. Narie's man fed her a story that persuaded her to say the cocaine belonged to her. She and I were arraigned and detained in what could be described as a barbaric correctional facility, Fox Hills. I tried to persuade Narie to tell the truth about who the cocaine belonged to because they were not at all interested in the stolen dress. I took responsibility for having stolen the dress, and was prepared to accept whatever consequences lay ahead. Narie refused to clear herself and pleaded guilty to the charge of narcotics possession and conspiracy to traffic abroad. I pleaded guilty to the charges of grand larceny. I let it be known that I was not taking the weight for the cocaine. Our accommodations were equivalent to something out of the movie *Midnight Express*. The barbaric accommodations would be my home for twenty seven days. It was a huge barn with no running water and a hole in the ground that served as a toilet for more than 30 women. The water bugs were as big as the palm of my hand. The mosquito's, whose bites lingered for days, quietly snuck upon you never making a sound. My only focus while I was there was to do whatever it took to get out. And I did just that! When time came for my second court appearance, I solicited the magistrate and was released in exchange for several sexual favors. He had my address and I made an agreement to join him for dinner and a show during his next trip to New York.

Sure enough he showed up for a convention for international law enforcement officers. I kept my end of the bargain and showed him a good time. So good a time, he fell asleep and I relieved him of all his currency foreign and domestic. In my mind I was compensating myself for the things that were stolen from my luggage during my imprisonment. I knew I was responsible for Narie being in that hole. The bottom line was that she made the decision to remain in that hell hole for six months rather than give up the chump she chose to call her man. Neither he nor I did anything for her the entire time she was incarcerated. I just prayed she would make it out. Some years later I did run into her so my prayers were answered.

I returned to New York a very grateful and happy camper. I made my rounds to find out what was going on in the city since my incarceration in the Bahamas. I discovered my dear friend and patron, Stoney had passed away from a massive heart attack. I suspect his cause

Poetic Recovery

of death was attributed to having ingested to much cocaine. Yes, that's right. He enjoyed eating spoonfuls of the white powder, while he sat on the side of the bed with a mirror and a bucket of water between his legs a precaution should the police visit. He would play the role of a film director and watch live sexual performances between women and couples he arranged with his woman Marlene and me. Marlene and I always had big fun together, and genuinely enjoyed each other's company. We talked about everything, current events, world news, business and pleasure. (Good cocaine will make you talk or paranoid) Marlene was smart and never squandered her money, and Stoney gave her plenty of it. He was never judgmental and paid big money for services rendered. Marlene's brother Darrius often showed up on special occasions when Stoney's palate required something a little more risque. Darrius was a beautiful boy whose ability to pick pockets placed him in high demand by hustlers who played the shot (pick pockets). It was common knowledge if you went to work with Darrius you were going to get paid. Darrius was a chameleon who could slide in and out of any establishment undetected. Stoney demanded that all participants have fun, follow directions and by all means hold nothing back. Every date with Stoney was a "Trip" and he is greatly missed.

Life Don't Rhyme

Chapter Thirty Six

My mother still lived in the same apartment on the Grand Concourse. It was located directly across the street from a nursing home whose workers were on strike. This was a perfect opportunity for me to get a job. I created a resume, gathered my courage and crossed the picket line. I was hired on the spot as a health care attendant. I took care of elderly patients whose families could no longer care for them at home. I spent time reading and talking to the patients who were often alone and suffering from various ailments, in addition to old age and dementia. Because the strikers were angry, I wouldn't risk going home so I'd sleep over most nights because overtime was being approved. It was becoming increasingly hard to smoke crack on that job, however that didn't keep me from trying. I left that job after three weeks without incident. This experience confirmed I would never allow my parents to be placed in the care of people who did not genuinely love them or at the very least respect them. Still needing a source of income, I ran into a friend, Cid with whom I sold dope, on Seventh Avenue and 112th Street. There was a small bar on the corner of the downtown side that provided a heroin clientele that was non-stop. Ultimately the owners grew tired of the police running in and out of their establishment and shut down the bar. Cid informed me that he was

Poetic Recovery

traveling to Augusta Georgia where his step children were living. Their mother, his ex had been sentenced to 45 years for the sale and distribution of heroin and cocaine. Because I was acquainted with Cid's ex, it came as no surprise that her mouth had written a check her ass couldn't cash, in the state of Georgia no less. Cid explained he was going to take a shot at selling drugs on the road and wanted to know if I wanted to travel with him. I was confident that I would make some money doing two things, selling my ass and selling dope. Cid assured me that all my money was my money. As my options were limited, I packed a suitcase, ready to embark on yet another drug drenched journey. Our first stop was Fayetteville, North Carolina where I worked Fort Bragg's army base, the next stop was South Carolina's Camp LeJeune where I continued to work and make money. This trip confirmed one very important fact, wherever sex is sold, the sale of narcotics is running a close second. I did well in both areas. Upon our arrival in Augusta, Georgia we found Cid's step children still living in the house their mother had rented before her conviction. Cid's step daughter was fifteen years old, with a child. His step son was a young man whose teenage years had been severely infected and interrupted by negative behaviors and absence of his mother. These children looked to Cid as the savior who would restore their lives and return their status of the children of drug dealers with plenty of money. I was not going to be the one to tell them they were now average kids who may have to submit to going to school and working legal jobs. Cid had a cousin with whom he and I would be living. He didn't trust having drugs inside the same house with his stepchildren. What he didn't know was that his cousin's daughter had a baby and a baby's daddy who was a grimy undercover dope fiend. He was complete with drama and a reputation for being scandalous throughout Augusta. Because of the quantity of narcotics we were traveling with, it made sense not to keep it in our possession while on the road. Cid thought the drugs would be safe in his cousin's home. Boy oh boy was he wrong. Our clientele consisted of pimps and prostitutes who were working the army bases and of course the soldiers who protected our nation.

    On the morning Princess Diana married Prince Charles, Cid received a phone call. It was from his cousin, she informed him that his drugs had been stolen. While she relayed this news I was lying in the bed watching the festivities in England, and smoking crack. He calmly put the phone back in its cradle and walked over to the bed where I lay and slapped the pipe out of my hand, then proceeded to slap fire out of me. It wasn't until one of his partners who was in the room pulled him off of me that he repeated what had been told to him while on the phone. He had been told I had enlisted the services of his cousin's daughter and her baby's daddy to steal

Poetic Recovery

all the dope. It was said I intended to split it up when I returned to Augusta. This was all a total lie, yet Cid believed every word. I realized that if I was going to stay alive I would have to formulate a plan that would allow me to escape. The ass whooping I received took place on the highway from Fayetteville North Carolina to Augusta Georgia. Upon our arrival, in Augusta I continued to profess my innocence although it wasn't doing me a bit of good. Cid began questioning everyone in his cousin's house brandishing a 9 millimeter pistol the entire time. What he learned was that it was possible that someone else may have had the opportunity to rob him other than me. Common sense must have taken a few days off, because it never occurred to Cid that I had been with him during the time his drugs were stolen. Daaaaaa go figure! I was informed that we were returning to Fayetteville where I would begin working; to replace the dope that had been stolen. The one thing I had not been asked to do, was give up any of the money I had made from sexual services rendered. That was the main reason I decided to take the trip. Cid wasn't then, nor has he ever been a pimp. Though I was in pain, I knew I was not going to allow anyone to sell my ass for any purpose other than my own personal gain. As we began our trip back to Fayetteville Cid decided to stop and pick up a few items in a store. What he did next can only be described as divine intervention, because he left the keys in the ignition. It was at that moment I decided it was time for me to drive, having only been given a permit in Los Angeles I figured it was a good time to give it shot. When I knew he was in the store, I got behind the wheel and took off. I drove the car straight to the downtown Augusta police station and parked it in their parking lot. I proceeded to call my father, who came to the rescue with a bus ticket to Fayetteville. I returned to Fayetteville, without incident and went straight to work. I made enough money for a motel room, food, a couple of outfits and of course more crack cocaine. Two days later, Cid arrived in Fayetteville, where he found me in a club where I was working the boys in uniform. He sent me a drink, and came over to the bar where I was sitting. He apologized for not believing me and said, he had found the culprit. He also said he was still angry about one thing; I had misrepresented myself by not telling him I knew how to drive. Of course he was stupid enough to ask me if we could resume our relationship. My response was hell no!

    I remained in Fayetteville for a couple of weeks after that. I would have remained longer had I not tried to solicit the only black police sergeant in the town. He was like most plain clothed officers I had run into through the years. Crooked! All he wanted was, to be serviced. He did take time to tell me about his ex-wife who left him for, wouldn't you know it, a pimp and some crack. Having listened to his sob story, he paid me and took me straight to the bus station and

Poetic Recovery

put me on a bus headed back to New York. I got off the bus and went to a different motel where I worked long enough to bum a ride back to New York with a nice truck driver who smoked my one and only love, crack
cocaine. I learned while under the influence of an illicit drug, healthy decision making goes right out the window. Healthy relationships do not exist when you are in the grips of active
addiction. Crack cocaine did nothing other than contaminate my mind and deteriorate my quality of life. I learned that what I am not able to do for myself God can do. What I needed was the desire to stop using and that desire was no where in sight.

Life Don't Rhyme

On The Road Again

Poetic Recovery

Chapter Thirty Seven

My next opportunity to get some fast money came in the form of a marriage proposition. However I had to travel to London England again. The groom was from Punjab India and his family resided in Queens.
I was paid five thousand dollars up front and a promise of another five thousand when
his citizenship was finalized. The family of the groom also provided round trip airfare and hotel accommodations. I purchased a pipe and an ample amount of cocaine which I cooked myself before my trip. Upon boarding the airline I lied and informed the stewardess that I was pregnant and experiencing morning sickness. I then asked her if she would mind if I utilized the restroom in first class so as not to inconvenience the passengers in coach. I must have been very convincing because she believed me to the point that she re-assigned me to a seat in the first class section of the plane. I smoked crack on the plane throughout the entire flight undetected. I could get up anytime and utilize the bathroom, without inconveniencing any of the other passengers. You could smoke
cigarettes on the planes back then so I had no problem. I can honestly say I had taken getting high to another altitude, with total disregard for the safety of other passengers. Upon my arrival to Heathrow Airport I dismantled my crack pipe, carefully placing the mouth piece and stem in the

hem of my skirt. I had been smoking crack nonstop for seven hours. The bowl of the crack pipe had turned a golden brown from the residue of the cocaine. Residue is just as potent as crack and can also be smoked. Lucky for me the residue was the same color I had my hair braided and because I knew I would need to touch it up I brought along extra braids. It was these extra braids I placed in the bowl of my crack pipe in order to get it through customs. My bowl had become a braid holder and I came through customs without a second thought.

My future husband was at least 35 years my senior. He was short with a repulsive body order that screamed he was not acquainted with soap and water and wanted to be alone. For the most part I enjoyed my trip due to the family owning their own silk import and export business. They were generous and allowed me to pick and choose from an array of garments they manufactured.

Having depleted my supply of crack cocaine I substituted it for over proof rum and remained a functional drunk throughout my stay. There was no way I would risk searching for cocaine in London not after the Bahamas experience. I figured after my first trip to London I was not going to risk alerting Interpol of my presence. The moment we were married we went back to my hotel room where I realized I wasn't the only person consuming rum. My husband became crazed and obsessed with his

Poetic Recovery

desire to consummate the marriage. This was not part of the deal and more importantly his family had not given him any form of currency. This made my goodies non-negotiable, no money, no honey. I was forced to lock myself in the bathroom for the night. The next morning I crept out of the bathroom and found my new husband gone. It was then I concocted another believable story that would speed up my departure and return me to New York and my lover Crack! The story began with one of my many imaginary children having been injured in a car accident. The child needed surgery and I was required to return to New York immediately. I don't have a clue as to what ever happened to this husband. I did receive a letter in the mail informing me the marriage had been annulled.
I learned that greed is fed by the greed of others. It is also safe to say that I had little or no regard for the sanctity of marriage.

Life Don't Rhyme

Chapter Thirty Eight

Upon my return to New York I was pleased to learn my mother had moved once again. This time she moved into a very nice apartment complex, the Lionel Hampton Houses in Harlem. My oldest brother Kenan was married to his high school sweetheart Reyna. They had a baby girl Monya; and would soon give birth to a son Kenan Jr. My brother Darien was beginning college and had also begun his family with a beautiful baby girl, Torrie. Brandon having graduated was working and living at home with my sister's Allana and Rachelle. Both were in school and growing into beautiful teenagers. My mother had been blessed to find and fall in love with a wonderful man who accepted her and her children without question. They had been living together in the apartment on the Grand Concourse and decided to take their relationship to a higher level. They were both working, he for New York State Parole and she for New York Criminal Justice Department. During my return home, I discovered that Rachelle had picked up a few of my traits leading toward her new found independence. She continued to deal with Sol and for all intents and purposes was very well taken care of. She remained in school and was seriously studying modern dance, in addition to studying the opposite sex. My mother still not understanding the magnitude of my addiction told me to get a job right away, if I had any intentions of living under her roof. I was all for trying to do the right thing. At the time my options were few. It occurred to me that I had always taken care of my brothers and sisters and knew everything about running a house. It was at that moment I thought I would do well as a live-in nanny. I landed a job after having forged references from my mother. It was easy since she and I did not share the same last name. The reference letter said that my previous employer was a judge and that I had taken care of her and her family since she was married, in addition to caring for her three children from birth.

    The job I was applying for was for the daughter of the then owner of a famous hotel in Las Vegas, Nevada. He was also the CEO for a railroad corporation. When they checked references I answered the phone giving myself an outstanding recommendation. I was hired right after Christmas. I had been getting high the night before the day I was to report for my first day of work. At that time I still owned a genuine Louis Vuitton duffel bag, not a knock off like the ones they sell today. I was crossing the street at 59th Street and First Avenue when a yellow cab came past me so fast that it ripped the bag in half. At that moment I knew I was in no condition to take care of anyone, especially children. However that did not deter me from my purpose. The family I was to work for were conveniently skiing in Aspen. However they had house guests whom I would be looking after in their absence. I was assigned a beautiful room complete with full bath, cable and a view overlooking the 59th Street Bridge. If nothing else I could cook gourmet meals without a recipe no matter how high I got. The first opportunity that arose I conducted a thorough search of the apartment. I found the keys to the jewelry drawer in a dressing table in the bedroom. I also located the furs hanging in the front closet. With New Year's Eve approaching I picked that day as being perfect for a robbery. My disease of addiction surpassed all morals and principals. I packed all the furs, and the remainder of the jewelry I hadn't yet sold off during the first week on job in the 47th Street Diamond District. I also packed a few pieces of clothing I liked neatly in two available suitcases. I then informed the doorman that my employer had instructed me to take them to the airport, where they would be flown to Aspen. Without question the doorman went to the street and hailed a cab, for which he was nicely tipped.

In my haste to leave the apartment I forgot the Louis Vuitton bag that had been ripped in half by the taxi my first day on the job. It contained all of my identification. And of course, I also left my set of keys inside the apartment. At that moment another bright idea attacked my brain instructing me to send my youngest sister Allana who was a minor, to my job the next day to retrieve the bag. The moment she arrived she was detainedby the police until my mother came to pick her up from the local precinct. My mother

Poetic Recovery

lost her job and what was worse she had become fed up with me and my mess.

This was the most drama I had ever taken my mother or anyone in my family through. This drama became a high profile case and caused me to have to leave New York until the statute of limitations was up. Money could not fix the pain I had put my mother through. I discovered that the love my mother had for me was truly unshakable and unconditional. She explained that she loved me however she did not like the creature I had become. She told me she would continue to pray that her princess would return before it became too late.

I sold off the furs and some of the jewelry before I left to go South. I remembered having met two women in jail in the Bahamas who were also locked up for trafficking. It amazes me, even now, that I had enough sense to network, even in that hell hole. We had exchanged numbers and promised to look each other up if we were ever in each other's area. Based on my recent activities, I figured a visit would be right on time. First, I had to get out of New York. I began with buying a wig to alter my appearance. I dressed shabbily and added a physical impairment that made me appear as if I had suffered a stroke. On the day I left New York I was on Eighth Avenue where I spotted my mother and walked right past her. She didn't recognize me and that confirmed in my mind that I truly had mastered my disguise. There is no doubt that had she recognized me she would have turned me into the police herself.

I went to the Port Authority and got on the first bus headed South. I had my pipe and a substantial amount of crack with me. My first stop was Fayetteville, North Carolina where I had visited and worked previously with Cid. During that trip I was kidnapped and repeatedly raped. It was my quick thinking combined with prayer and an Academy Award winning performance of someone having an asthma attack that led to my survival. Having scared my captors into taking me to an emergency room it was as we were exiting the elevator in the lobby of the Fayetteville Sheraton that I met a gambler who came to my rescue. He would be the only person I would contact during this impromptu trip. I checked into the Executive Motel on Hay Street and proceeded to find my once upon a time savior, "Big Man." It made perfect sense to me that since I would be in town, I may have need of his resources. Hay Street continued to be the strip where the soldiers from Fort Bragg frequented when given passes for R and R (rest and relaxation). I took advantage of every soldier that wanted to spend some money while leaving messages in places I knew Big Man frequented informing him that I was in town. Finally Big Man surfaced. He called me instructing me to meet him in the back of the pool room on Hay Street where he was gambling. I found him easily and told him a story

Poetic Recovery

about needing to leave New York as a result of an abusive relationship. There was no way I would divulge any information concerning the robbery. I informed him I had some dope I needed to move and that I was on a schedule to leave Fayetteville in three days. I utilized him to help me get rid of the dope. He didn't want money for his trouble, he wanted sex. Whew what a relief! I knew that would be the easiest form of payment I would ever have to make because all it entailed was that I lay there. I had long since stopped enjoying sex under those conditions. My orgasms were given to me through the stem of a glass pipe. I was able to pawn a couple pieces of jewelry while I in Fayetteville, fattening up my bankroll. When the time was right I took off for Fort Lauderdale Florida.

    I called Belinda, whom I had met while locked up in the Bahamas Fox Hills Correctional Facility. I told her I was coming to see her, and that I would pay her to stay in her home rather than a hotel. I took the bus because I was still paranoid about the New York robbery and didn't want to take any chances in the airports, not to mention I couldn't stop smoking the crack long enough to get on any other form of transportation. When I arrived I was greeted by Belinda and her girlfriend Cat at the bus station. Both were as hospitable as tour guides. When the cash flow slowed down Belinda got me a job as barmaid, in a local haunt that sold good cocaine. When you live in another person's house it is never quite comfortable getting high there. I stayed in the window and next to the door more than any other place in the house. I was constantly checking for the police. Crack caused me to become severely paranoid. I worked long enough to take a sting (robbery), after which I was soon fired and no longer a welcomed guest. The money had finally run out and it was time to go, but where? I had no more jewelry left. What I needed was a job and a new crack pipe.

Strange, how creative addicts are in their addiction. It was in Miami that I learned the art of smoking crack from a beverage can. Unbelievable!

Poetic Recovery

Chapter Thirty Nine

I moved from Fort Lauderdale, to Miami where I decided I would go to work as an exotic dancer. Though I had taken ballet lessons as a child they didn't prepare me for the reception I would receive when taking off my clothes on stage in front of a bunch of strangers. I was in my early thirties by this time. I was fairly young, with no visible scars yet. I had always been gifted with the ability to speak, and there was no time like the present to put this tool to work. My addiction was in command. I really couldn't stop smoking crack alone, and my ego would not allow me to admit I was anything other than a narcotics consumer.

I found myself doing some very nasty things in some very nasty places. It was during these times that I chose to call on God. The moment I got into serious trouble I'd scream his name, and he always came through for me. I had been taught my entire life that he may not come when you call him, but he's always on time. As an active ungrateful addict nothing is ever fast enough. Somehow I found my way to an establishment where they were always hiring called The Mint. God had been good to me, my body had not been scarred or ravaged by my drug use. I still managed to eat daily no matter how high I got. I convinced myself that eating would allow me to come down from the previous high causing my body to feel the affect of the next hit of crack. Compared to the other dancers I was the least talented. The one talent I did possess, that many did not, was the ability to talk a man out of his money. Not to say my co-workers didn't get money, because they did. However, it was the manner in which I presented myself that placed me in a category all by myself. I put my gift to gab, my smile, and my ability to gyrate my hips together to create a performance worthy of receiving nightly tips in excess of over three hundred dollars nightly. I was fortunate enough to make the acquaintance of a real estate agent who offered me an opportunity to purchase a townhouse right across the street from where I was currently dancing. What he wanted in exchange was what everyone wanted, sex which I was more than willing to provide. He created a veterans loan for me. Hell, the closest I had ever been to a veteran was the dates I had during my days at Camp Lejune and Fort Bragg. The mortgage was cheap and I would have no problem paying it with the money I was making nightly. I didn't question any of the arrangements he made for securing the mortgage. I wasn't using my real name anyway so it didn't matter. I was Joan Tyler, and I for one knew the name was clean because it belonged to a woman whom I sat next to on one of my trips. When he took me to the house I was shocked. The town house was brand new with a garage, two bedrooms, two baths, and front and back yards. The business

Poetic Recovery

woman in me told me to get a roommate to ensure I always had the mortgage payment on time. I went through two roommates who had too much drama of their own. I found the necessary men in the drug game I needed to keep me supplied, which left me under the impression that my life was good. I ate daily, shopped regularly and had costumes made to order for work.

    I ran into some characters that worked jobs and just wanted an occasional date. However, there were some customers who wanted me to travel for the purpose of carrying drugs. I took advantage of the trips because the destinations were all in the states. Of course I paid myself first before venturing into parts unknown. There was one trip to Toledo Ohio I took with a father and son team. Once we arrived in Toledo we went to the home of some friends of the son. Everyone was sitting around relaxing, drinking, getting acquainted and of course sniffing and smoking cocaine. The son an ex Marine, disappeared into the bathroom on the first floor for what seemed like more than an hour. All of a sudden water came pouring into the living room from the bathroom. Apparently the son had been shooting pure cocaine. He shot so much of it he became crazed. He pulled the toilet up out of the floor and the sink from the wall with his bare hands all of this while the water was on. His father took it all in stride. He paid for the damages, delivered the cocaine to

Life Don't Rhyme

the customers that were expecting him and returned to Miami. Florida was filled with characters that made my addictive behaviors look angelic. I was getting high to the point I was fired from my job as a dancer at the Mint. I had become pathetic and unable to keep the job that was conveniently located across the street from my house. I couldn't keep that glass dick out of my mouth long enough to do my damn job or save my life. It was my birthday and though I had no job celebrating took priority
because it gave me a legitimate reason to smoke crack. I was dating another married man, who was employed until we met. He cleaned out his checking account and the joint savings account he shared with his wife. For thirty days and thirty nights we smoked crack nonstop. It was insane!

On the last night he decided to rent his truck out to a crack dealer. It was the only transportation we had. Aside from the crack, the dealer threw in a carton of Newport cigarettes and a case of Heineken beer. He then dropped us off at my house, saying he would return the vehicle the next day. He never returned. Before this adventure in Florida was over, I would buy and sell three vehicles for crack cocaine. The insanity of my addiction dragged me through the gutter of every city I set foot in. My disease had no problem traveling because it knew where ever I went, it went with me.

Poetic Recovery

Chapter Forty

Of course crack didn't allow me to blame myself for my loss of employment. Crack convinced me that it was time for a change. I began renting out the bedrooms in my house to the dancers across the street. They utilized the rooms to further entertain customers between sets. This arrangement worked for awhile. What I hadn't counted on was my next door neighbor being a Miami Dade police officer from Pittsburg Pennsylvania. This meant I had to go into the city to look for work. What's worse I didn't have a car so I hitchhiked. I went straight to Biscayne Boulevard. It was a popular area in Miami for the sex trade. Prostitutes, pimps, strip joints and peep shows lined both sides of the boulevard. Opportunity was waiting for anyone as long as they could take off their clothes. I worked two clubs on the strip, and as usual, lost the jobs due to continued drug use.

I met many people from all walks of life, devoted to the lifestyle of peddling flesh, and drugs. I was close to becoming homeless when I met a brazen thief, Donald. Donald's area of expertise was taking cash registers he couldn't open. I had a collection of keys from my earlier capers with Marlow, so it worked out fine. Donald was able to turn the lights and water on in the townhouse for awhile. I also took advantage of making money from parking cars in my driveway when there was a game at the

Life Don't Rhyme

Robbie Stadium across the street. Business was good for a couple of years due to the Super Bowls being played there, in addition to regular football games and concerts. I made as much as two hundred dollars parking one recreational vehicles. I was able to park four vehicles per event in my personal parking spaces. Donald made out fine because he washed and robbed the vehicles for their contents. I began losing a lot of my clientele because I was stealing from them too.

    Soon thereafter I lost the town house and moved into another house my real estate agent had available. He became my knight in shining armor. It didn't take long before those who wanted to find me did because selling sex is as much a commodity as any stock on Wall Street. I was always meeting new dates, many who were from out of town, which proved to be in my favor since I always crept in their pockets and they never returned to confront me. I continued getting high and frequented an area in Miami called Opalocka to buy my drugs. I had pretty much been blackballed from working in any strip joints as it was rumored that I was a crack head and a thief. Rumors didn't faze me because
the fact remained that I truly needed a job.

    I hooked up with a man, Cashmere, who was as smooth and soft spoken as his name. His area of expertise was B&E (breaking and entering). I continued to live in the same area where I once owned the townhouse which made me familiar with the shift changes of the Dade County Police. I realized very early, in life thanks to my father, that I had no future in being a thief that is I was never cut out to go into stores and take merchandise in clear view. My addiction however convinced me to put forth an effort anyway. Two out of three times I was busted and sent to jail. So that ended that career choice. With Cashmere, I felt comfortable going into the homes of people who were once my neighbors and taking their property while they were not at home. I received orders from customers mostly drug dealers who often bought the merchandise Cashmere and I had stolen. During the Christmas season I received an order for a playground set. I lowered myself to go into a day care center in a local church and steal all the toys and a complete jungle gym just so I could smoke crack alone on Christmas Day. I had sunk to a new low. Breaking into homes went well for a good six months before we both got busted. While in Miami I always kept in touch with my mother, though I couldn't speak to her on the phone for a long period of time because the New York police continued to have the phone tapped due to the robbery. I let her know that I was now locked up in Florida and that she should take this time to rest in knowing I was alive and safe. I was sentenced to six months for breaking and entering and possession of stolen property. This jail time didn't do me a bit of good. When I was released I was homeless, with nowhere to live and less than twenty dollars in my pocket. I made one attempt to get into a drug treatment program and I was informed that I was not fucked up enough to be allowed into the program. I immediately spent what money I did have on crack so I could get high. I ran into someone who had a tool shed he had converted into a studio apartment. I lived with him for approximately one week after which I couldn't stand it any longer and called my mother for a ticket to come back home one more time. I know now that it was the power of those prayers said by my mother and other people that brought me out of Miami unharmed. It was my cries to God to help deliver me out of my mess, that softened the heart of mymother enough to provide a bus ticket so that could give living life on life's terms another try. What I failed to understand was that I had to turn my will over in order to make this change. Turning my will over was something I was not knowingly willing to do. No matter how badly I wanted to square up, stop smoking crack, and get a job. However, my disease of addiction let me believe I could do all those things and still smoke crack. I still didn't understand who was in charge, and my addiction continued to tell me that I was.

Chapter Forty One

It wasn't easy being in my mother's house again. She was still in the same relationship with Josh. He was a wonderful man who adored her. He genuinely cared about my mother and her children. I knew it the moment we met. More importantly he was an ex-drug addict who was now a counselor. This intrigued me, because I was interested as to how he had gotten his life together. My brother Darien was still in college. Brandon and, Rachelle had moved out and Allana was still at home attending high school. I was permitted to sleep on the couch. The couch was a luxury after being homeless in Miami. My mother told me not to get comfortable because she was making arrangements for me to enter into a drug treatment program and I said I would go. Mommy's new man Josh informed me that he had just the place for me. The only delay was, I had to wait for a bed. Immediately, my disease of addiction began speaking to me in my own voice, telling me I was running out of time. It told me I had better get as high as I could before I went into the program, and that is exactly what I set out to do. I made my rounds and hit up everyone I knew. I told them I had been locked up and was just getting back on my feet. This line was standard when anyone had not been seen in a while. It guaranteed me a free high. The day arrived when it was time to go into the treatment program. When I arrived for the interview a tall brown skinned man dressed in a suit, instructed me to be seated. I examined his every movement and his tone of his voice as he explained the nature of the questions he would be asking me. He began with when were you born, how old are you, what religion do practice, do you love your parents etc? Then he asked had I ever caused bodily harm to another human being? I responded "no, and furthermore, unless I have a lawyer present I will not continue to answer any more questions on that subject." He stopped abruptly and said "this interview is over."

    I knew they would not permit me into the program because I lacked the willingness to disclose information that was pertinent to the intake process. The two reasons that would keep a person from being admitted into treatment programs were; they had been convicted of a sexual offense or a violent crime. However, Josh did not give up trying to find a treatment facility that would accept me into its program. He made a few more calls and sure enough another program responded to his call. They told him a bed had become available.

    On the day I was scheduled to go into the program, I was turned away from the door due to the facility being under quarantine for smallpoxs. The news of this epidemic caused me to indulge myself in the consumption of crack for a little while longer. When my mother got wind of my not being able to go somewhere other than her house, she strongly suggested that I do something with myself right away. She explained to me that she could no longer sit and watch me kill myself, and that my lifestyle threatened her safety and her home. She concluded that one way conversation by telling me to leave her house. She said if I were hungry she would feed me, if I needed anything other than money she would provide it for me, but under no circumstances could I continue to live in her home and use crack. I couldn't blame her I had recently been busted by my brother Brandon trying to steal the big water bottle that was filled with change out the house between my legs.

    As badly as I knew I needed help I could not help myself. I took to living in the streets. I spent a lot of time at my girlfriend Doretta's house. Her mother, Mina was a saint who never turned anyone she loved away from her door. No matter what she heard about them she would let you in and feed you. If it was in the morning you were guaranteed a slice of pound cake and a cup of coffee. If it were at night you had whatever was cooking. Mina asked the same question of everyone she knew who was doing wrong. "When are you going stop this mess and get yourself together?" I could never find the words to answer Mina. Crack had left no one out. Everyone I knew was smoking free base and the funny thing is that it was by no means "free" it came with a high price. I began a routine of going to work daily from 8am to 4pm to play what is known as "the shot" or pick pockets.

Life Don't Rhyme

I worked with a guy by the name of Larry. He was straight with me for the most part. All I did was block the stairwell on the buses we rode. I was scared to death to put my hands into someone's pocket. This little tactic enabled Larry to dip into some unsuspecting Vic's pocket or pocket book, usually undetected. He always had credit cards and went to the banks for cash advances, after which we shopped and shopped. Much of the merchandise bought on credit cards was always sold for cash and drugs. It was important that all transactions on any one card be done within a certain timeframe. In most cases we were able to check whether or not it had been reported stolen. This career move was short lived because he was arrested by the bunko squad. This squad of detectives concentrated primarily on busting pick pockets or shot players and con-players.

      The day he was busted he was working with someone else because I was still getting high from the day before and could not be found. I took his arrest to be a warning for me not to work with anyone else. Most pick pockets were dealing with another sort of demon called chasing the dragon. This was heroin being added to crack and then smoked. The primary drug of choice of many shot players is heroin or P-funk. I had enough to deal with trying to smoke up Peru, and had no intention of being disloyal to my drug of choice, cocaine. I know now that it is only by the grace of God that heroin never

Poetic Recovery

appealed to me. It was because of the damage it did to the body that discouraged me from ever wanting to use it. Even as a crack head I was vain in that respect. However, I found out that what I was, was in denial. I had always been a healthy size twelve, now I was a size six. I was now wearing two pairs of pants to make me appear bigger. I had a big head, sunken cheeks and my eyes resembled a deer caught in a windshield. I was truly one of the walking dead.

It is said, when all else fails do what you do best. At that point what I believed I did best was smoke crack. However no one was going to pay me to do that so all that was left was to sell my ass. It was time to come full circle. I returned to Park Avenue, no not near the Waldorf Astoria or even 87th Street, my old address so many years ago. It was upper Park Avenue under the Metro North, stretching from 110th Street to 135th street. This area was dominated by crack heads, dope fiends, drag queens, derelicts, and the lowest forms of pimps and prostitutes in existence. The sole purpose of this existence is to do nothing other than get high from one day to next. I gave a lot of thought to what a remarkable sense of humor God has. It would be close to six years before he allowed me to know that I was the brunt of the joke. Until then I was content to destroy myself and ignore all the signs that screamed stop!

Chapter Forty Two

      I was very conscious of the HIV problem and always used condoms. I got into the habit of being tested regularly. Back then they paid top dollar to test for the virus. That money always came in handy when I wanted to get high. The mobile medical unit gave out thousands of condoms. I always had enough to sell to the tricks and the working girls. I took that as another confirmation that my life had spiraled downhill. Yet I had no idea that I would be sinking a lot lower very soon. I discovered working those streets required I have protection. That usually meant you had to have a pimp. I was not about to take myself through that drama again. I was able to get around that by providing a local pimp I knew, with a bag of heroin and or a sexual favor. I knew he had a heroin habit and that it was less wear and tear on me if I just provided him with a bag of dope. I vowed once again that I wouldn't steal from my regular dates and I managed to keep that promise. However, no one informed me that I may encounter an occasional crazy date that would take my money and me. It wasn't unusual for a handsome guy in a nice car to pick up girls in this area. One night I thought I had picked up a nice guy. He said we were going to his house in Westchester County. He gave me a hundred dollars and of course my thirsty ass agreed to go. We arrived at a very nice house not far from the highway.

Poetic Recovery

I undressed and he called in his woman in to join us. She was nice and introduced herself. She made me a drink as we all got naked and became better acquainted, shortly after which she left the room. Then my host instructed me to lay on my stomach, which I did. All I felt were the teeth of a human being biting my back. It wasn't hard enough to break the skin, but hurt like hell and left marks. This went on until I was able to go into my old faithful asthma attack performance. God stepped in and he got scared and dropped me off at the emergency room of the nearest hospital. After that episode I began asking the other women about dates before I solicited anyone. If a date hadn't been with some of the other girls that could vouch for him I usually wouldn't go. The nights when it was slow, and I became thirsty all bets were off. I was ready to service Jack the Ripper then. With every risk I would pray I would be able to escape long enough to smoke some more crack.

After a year of being out there on Park Avenue, I became wise as to who was a date and who was a stick up kid or rapist. I had acquired some regular customers I had come to rely on. This meant I didn't steal from them because most times if I ran into them I could always get a couple of dollars until we scheduled a date. I made sure I was always clean and neatly dressed. I frequented the local thrift shops and found suitable clothing. I tried never to bother my mother with my nonsense though I did stop by to take a bath and wash my ass. And when I wasn't turning a date in a hotel, or jumping in and out of cars or turning dates in hallways, alley ways and parks I was given the blessing of deep sleep. I utilized the fire hydrant in the summer to wash my feet. When I couldn't camouflage my own funk any longer I would part with some crack to utilize anyone's shower or bath tub whenever possible. It was always a crack head who had managed to keep a roof over their head and wanted to smoke. I became known for giving up some of my crack for a bath and a beer, and not necessarily in that order. One summer day my mother was searching for me to let me know that my oldest brother Kenan and his new wife were in town and wanted to see me. When he saw me he broke down and cried at the sight that was once his big sister. I hadn't seen Kenan cry since I busted his head open on the bunk beds in his room at Daddy's house when we were children. His tears confirmed what I refused to accept; that I had become a sub-human, a junkie, a derelict, and a complete disgrace! He told me that the thing he was staring at couldn't possibly be his sister. He told me I needed to get help, and until I made up my mind to do so there was nothing he could or would do for me. I immediately got an attitude, and told him that he was wasting his time and that I wasn't hurting anyone other than myself. I continued to place my life at risk going in and out of Riker's Island Rose M Singer Women's House

Poetic Recovery

of Detention. When I wasn't in jail I was in another jail somewhere else in the country often in my hometown of Rochester New York being a further embarrassment to my father. I thought geographical changes would solve my problems and help me control my addiction. I seemed to always return to upper Park Avenue. While working on Park Avenue I met a young woman, Luci whose apartment I would frequent to get high in. She lived on 124th Street off Lenox Avenue. Her apartment was close enough to get to work on Park Avenue and far enough to get some uninterrupted sleep. She and I became great friends. I gave her money and got her high when I could and she did the same for me. She afforded me the use of her bathroom and apartment when I would catch a good date with money. I always made sure my dates paid her for her accommodations. One morning we were both broke and wanted to get high. I told her about the van that came around for HIV testing and more importantly that they paid. She and I got tested and paid. However to get paid a second time you had to return to receive your results. It was when we went back together for the results that Luci found out that she had tested positive for the virus. That was one of the darkest days of my life. There was nothing I could say to her without feeling guilty. Yet in the back of my mind I knew I had helped to save her life. The look on her face told me that she was in shock. Silence was the only sound between us.

Life Don't Rhyme

There is no such thing as needing a crack, but on that day I truly did. Approximately two weeks later after receiving this life changing news Luci got busted. She was charged and convicted for the sale of a controlled substance and sentenced to three to six years. With her apartment no longer accessible to me I needed somewhere to live. Going to my mother's house was out of the question. She and Josh had moved to Florida to concentrate on their marriage and to get away from my crack head ass. I took it upon myself to find a couple of customers that frequented Luci's apartment, Earnest and Hutch. I knew they lived somewhere in the neighborhood near 120th Street and Lenox Avenue. I also knew if I could locate them I would have shelter for awhile. I was one of the few women Luci allowed to remain in her apartment when those two men came to visit her. The secret to their many visits was that Luci was an excellent opponent when playing cards, especially a card game known as Coon-Can. They always arrived with many cracks and plenty of money to purchase more when those ran out. One of Luci's friends, Window Washer exchanged Earnest and Hutch's location for a date. I found out that Hutch owned a building known as central booking where Earnest was also tenant. When I found them I explained to Earnest and Hutch that Luci had been busted and that I needed somewhere to live. When I said I would be able to pay Earnest responded with "come on in and have a hit." I

Poetic Recovery

was shocked and happily surprised when Earnest said I could stay at his apartment and that all I had to do was give him some money when I had it. I was equally shocked that he didn't want any sex at the time. Earnest revived my memory telling me, I knew him when I worked as a barmaid in the *Big Track* for New York Willie and Herschel. My memory was mush and I figured that I could put it together as time progressed. We knew many of the same people so it was possible that our paths had crossed. However, he had changed since then, due to being severely burned in a fire. Over seventy five percent of his body had been disfigured. That didn't keep him from getting high. He was genuinely a nice guy however he was a gangster who could become lethal if provoked. Being in a fire never made him a victim it only fueled him to live and play that much harder and recklessly. Earnest lived on the 3rd floor and paid rent to Hutch. It was rumored that Hutch was the brother of an actress. I later found out it was true, but she didn't come anywhere near the building her brother owned. Hutch got high daily and enjoyed coming to Luci's house, because it meant no one could find him. Hutch was married to a woman who truly if given the opportunity could smoke her husband under the table. Hutch's building was infested with drug dealers who were paying him to sell narcotics out of his building. The building was nick named "central booking" because the police visited so often.

Life Don't Rhyme

Earnest and Hutch played cards daily as a form of leisure and profit. What they did most of the time was get high and talk shit. Because I didn't want to be looked upon as a free loader and didn't like having to ask anyone for anything, I continued to go to work on Park Avenue every day. Rarely would I return without cracks and money. Some nights and days were better than others and that didn't seem to bother Earnest at all. He still managed to smoke crack regardless. While living with Earnest I ran into many hustlers who would frown upon anyone smoking crack, only to be smoking it undercover in central booking themselves. It occurred to me that crack cost too much money not enjoy it so I refused to sneak, unless I didn't want to share my crack and went out of my way to take as many hits alone as possible. One good thing about being around men who smoked crack, it was guaranteed that they wanted sexual favors while smoking it. In my company it was common knowledge that you had to pay me. They did, and I always offered them the first hit. Doing this insured that I wouldn't have to do a damn thing because after inhaling that first hit, they were no longer able to participate in any sexual activity they had paid for. Most times they were too paranoid to speak and when they did they spoke in a whisper. This sight would tickle me to no end because it truly demonstrated they were the real tricks.

Poetic Recovery

Chapter Forty Three

Earnest never asked me for any money and he didn't have to, I just gave it to him if I had it. One thing was guaranteed; I always had cracks, which meant Earnest always smoked. Every day when I woke up Earnest made sure I had something to eat, cigarettes and cracks. This was preparation to assist me in getting ready for my daily adventures on Park Avenue. I figured now would be a good time to make Earnest my man. After which I found out I didn't need to leave the building to get paid unless I wanted to. This made it easier for Earnest to monitor the people coming in and out of the building who dropped in to smoke their cracks assuring him his cut. Earnest and Hutch had a great set up or so I thought. More importantly it kept me off the streets. There were enough crack heads coming in and out of the building to keep me working and getting high at least sixteen hours a day.

It is common knowledge among crack smokers that once you begin smoking no one wants to go outside to get more once they have run out. I never minded going to buy the drugs because that ensured I would certainly have more crack to smoke. Why? Because I would tap the bags, another common practice among crack heads. What was important to me was to keep my new patrons high and happy. I provided accommodations, women and cracks. I went to

Life Don't Rhyme

the ATM, the liquor store and more importantly I came back with exactly what I was sent for. I lived in this building for three years smoking crack from sun-up to sundown. During the middle of the month business of every kind slowed down, however this did not apply to the sale of crack cocaine. There were days I didn't go to sleep and would ask for what is known as a "wake up." This always struck me as odd, because how can you require a wake up if you haven't been asleep. I received wake ups from the pitchers who enlisted my services as a lookout. I alerted them to police presence. The apartment Earnest and I shared had a bird's eye view of Lenox Avenue. I could see five blocks north and south from my third floor window.

It was during the third year with Earnest that he decided we would sell drugs. We made money but we always paid ourselves first. It was really important that I be the best lookout. This meant that I had to be alert and I didn't want to risk Earnest going to jail. I became very skilled at tapping the healthy cracks we were selling. They were packaged in aluminum foil and were always healthy making it easy to remove a few rocks and still leave the package, looking healthy;more importantly keeping the customers flowing at a steady pace, coming back for more. It was a matter of life and death not to dip into the cracks to the point that the customers complained. Earnest worked for someone and it was the fear of being shot, stabbed or killed that ensured we

Poetic Recovery

didn't get greedy. No one ever went to jail on my watch. On the one day that I wasn't the lookout it was a tossup whether or not we would be visited by New York's finest. At this point there were at least three different crews that sold drugs in Hutch's building and they all paid rent to Hutch. When Earnest apartment deteriorated to the point that the bathroom was uninhabitable, we were forced to use the accommodations of neighbors, usually Hutch's apartment. There was always drama about who sold drugs and when. It was this drama that allowed me steal packages of crack from the workers. Some of these workers couldn't count without using their fingers and toes. I did succumb to a beating where I lost a tooth after having been snitched out. However that didn't deter me from my primary purpose of getting high. I found other crews to steal from. There was nothing Earnest could do to defend me when I did get caught. Earnest was out manned and without fire power. I always knew that I would eventually get caught and would have to pay the price. I though of these episodes as hazards of the workplace.
(Talk about rationalizing)

      Ike sold most of his product in Hutch's building and became one of my best customers. He paid me well for information concerning anyone selling in the building without his permission and of course for services rendered. By this time Hutch had lost all control over what was done in what once was his building.

Life Don't Rhyme

Earnest was busted twice in 1995 and didn't have to do any real jail time. In 1996 we both were busted, a month apart. We were charged with the sale of a controlled substance. I was sentenced to a city year (eight months) on Riker's Island, and Earnest three to six years. For the life of me I didn't take this interruption to be anymore than a time out to fatten up and think of a new way to do wrong differently. I was concerned about nothing other than how soon it would be before I could return to my beloved crack!

Poetic Recovery

Chapter Forty Four

    While on Riker's Island the only correspondence I had was with my mother. My emotions were all over the place. I knew I didn't want to return to Lenox Avenue. However, my disease of addiction had something else in mind. I had not yet suffered enough to want to stop getting high. Incarceration only served to throw me into a relationship I used to satisfy the void that existed from not being able to smoke crack. I met and married Julie in a Riker's Island ceremony. Our relationship stemmed from an unfulfilled need to be loved and accepted and of course very low self esteem. My involvement with females was limited to sex for hire. To become involved in anything serious was never a consideration. However, Julie changed all that. She was educated, and attentive to my needs. She touched my heart where it had never been touched. Since my self esteem was as busted as my appearance; for her to pay attention to me sent my libido to go into overdrive. While on Riker's Island we worked on the same work detail and saw each other daily. I was assigned to cook for the guards in the laundry where she worked the machines. Whatever the guards ate, I prepared the same meals for Julie. Julie had been locked up for a violation of parole from a previous charge. She was being sent back up North to prison, for six months. We promised each other we would write to one another during our separation daily. She promised when she came home, she would come and visit me on Riker's Island. I wrote to her faithfully, and because we were both inmates we were not permitted to correspond with one another so I mailed the letters to her mother to forward. I never believed that Julie could have possibly been serious about being in a relationship with someone she had met in jail, so I figured I would just play it out and see where the relationship would lead. Sure enough she stayed true to her word and visited me. When I was released she invited me home to meet her mother who was a Christian. I knew from our first meeting she didn't condone her daughter's lifestyle. She was a lovely woman with her own truths and beliefs. Reluctantly she did accept me as her daughter's partner. Our life together during this period was turbulent. We both had reservations about returning to our active addictions. When those reservations surfaced, we became a volatile combination. We resorted back to our old attitudes and behaviors and ventured back into our old neighborhoods where we got high. We rekindled those negative relationships that contributed to the disease of addiction. I learned through an explosive demonstration that not only was Julie a crack head, but she was also a raging alcoholic. I never cared for alcoholics and after a few demonstrations by Julie while under the influence of alcohol, she confirmed one of the major reasons our relationship dissolved. I

Poetic Recovery

knew we could not survive as a couple and we certainly could not continue to get high together, because it was waste. I left, and we kept in touch until she eventually went back to prison. Little did I know I would follow close behind her. We would attempt to reunite seven years later for a dose of dysfunctional sobriety. What I learned from this relationship was, there is no place for love to grow when the only nourishment is an addiction; be it shopping or gambling. I learned I am not willing to change who I am for the acceptance of someone else, no matter how comfortable the living accommodations are. I learned it is alright to leave people where they are if being around them is going to diminish who I have become or disturb my serenity and peace of mind. Living a healthy lifestyle is key when living in recovery.

Life Don't Rhyme

STILL A ROSE

I TOLD EVERYONE THAT IT WAS JUST A
RUMOR I COULDN'T POSSIBLY BE, A
NARCOTICS CONSUMER
A NARCOTICS CONSUMER IS SIMPLY AN
ADDICT
A PERSON NO LONGER IN CONTROL,
WITH A VERY BAD HABIT.
A HABIT THAT ENABLES ME TO LEAP IN AND
OUT OF PERSONALITIES AT A SINGLE BOUND,
AS QUICKLY AS I CAN SMILE, I CAN FROWN.
FASTER THAN A SPEEDING BULLET,
NOW HEAR THIS
"UNDER THE INFLUENCE OF CRACK YOU ARE
NOT ALWAYS A SUCCESSFUL LIAR
I DIDN'T BELIEVE IT UNTIL THE GUN WAS
FIRED.
MORE POWERFUL THAN A LOCOMOTIVE,
ONLY WHEN UNDER THE INFLUENCE.
AT THAT TIME I WAS HIGH ENOUGH TO
BELIEVE
I WAS INDEED A SUPER HUMAN BEING
WHAT I HAD BECOME COULD ONLY BE
DESCRIBED AS SUB-HUMAN
SUDDENLY HERE I AM, HANDCUFFED AGAIN
GOING RIGHT BACK TO WHERE I HAVE
ALREADY BEEN
WHEN WILL I MAKE THE RIGHT CHOICE?
WHEN WILL I MAKE A COMMITMENT TO END
THIS MISSION OF DEATH?
SO THAT MY LIVING WILL NOT BE I VAIN

Poetic Recovery

Chapter Forty Five

My choices of where I could live were dwindling. My brothers had their own families and were not having anything to do with me while I was still active in my addiction.
My sister Rachelle and her daughter Brie were in Florida with my mother. However my baby sister Allana and I had always managed to have a decent relationship. So I turned to her. She worked a job and sold crack cocaine on the side to make her life and the lives of her children comfortable. She permitted me to live with her as a live in baby-sitter. It really was a great idea; however, my addiction took first priority over everything. I neglected her children and stole from her. My sister really tried her best to accommodate my habit as if anyone could. Needless to say, it was never enough. I mean go figure, would South America be enough for a crack head? When Allana could no longer feed my addiction or tolerate my behavior she put an end to our arrangement. She made an attempt to get me some help, by suggesting I check myself into a detox at Harlem Hospital.
Fat chance!
I went straight to find someone to get me high and stayed gone for two days, after which I was homeless again and left to my own devices. This was an ideal time to re-visit 193 Lenox Avenue aka central booking again. Though Earnest remained in prison, I still had a card I

had not played. During the time Earnest and I lived together in Hutch's building, we befriended an older man whose name was Charlie.

Charlie had a job and went to work faithfully no matter how high he got. He was a day laborer who worked on Seventh Avenue in the garment district. Charlie was sixty years old when we first met on Park Avenue years ago. One night Charlie came to the apartment I shared with Ernest and never left. He was 5' 5", light skinned, with grey hair. Charlie was an elderly giant. He didn't take any mess and would give you his last penny and his last crack. Charlie had remained in the apartment throughout mine and Earnest incarceration. It was with Charlie I would live after leaving my sister's house. Allana and Charlie shared a special relationship because he always had some type of money. Charlie had stopped smoking crack while I was away so there was never any drama going on in his apartment. More importantly he could be counted on to spend his money. He welcomed me back, and let me know that he could no longer work due to his failing health. Charlie told me he no longer smoked cracks because he was suffering from an array of ailments. Of course I was devastated. First, because that meant I was going to have to revert to selling my ass again. Secondly, I was going to have to seriously lookout for Charlie, because he was now taking medication and getting a monthly social security check. Charlie

Poetic Recovery

always liked the company of a female he could give instructions to when he was smoking crack. Now that he could no longer smoke crack cocaine it was important that sexual encounters fill that void. It was the friendship he and Earnest shared that wouldn't allow him to ask me for sexual favors. He would enlist me to go out and find someone suitable to perform the services he had come to enjoy under the influence of crack cocaine. Charlie was the sweetest man. He allowed me to conduct my business from his home. My sister Allana and I continued to do business together. However, it was Charlie who kept the money and the crack. My sister was not playing any games with her business or me. She was out for the money and was not accepting any shorts. I was the one responsible for selling her cracks. She allowed me to conduct all sales for which I was paid. I also turned dates and negotiated business for other narcotics consumers who dropped in. This living arrangement between Charlie and I was ideal. I inquired to Hutch about Earnest and when he would be released from prison.
Someone told me he had sent word that he would return home by Thanksgiving of 1998. Charlie seemed to choose when I was getting high to ask me "are you going to stop smoking that shit when Ernest comes home?" Only after I exhaled my smoke would I answer his question. The answer always being "yes" and that was a lie! I had no intentions of discontinuing my

relationship with the most wonderful glass dick in the world just because Ernest was coming home from prison. I was falling deeper and deeper into the bowels of addiction. I saw no end in sight. The day arrived when Earnest came home from prison, it was the day before Thanksgiving. Ernest walked through the door only to find me in the same familiar position he last saw, as he was being handcuffed and hauled away to jail two years earlier. My lips were wrapped around the stem of a glass pipe and I was sucking the cloud into my lungs that formed in the bowl of my crack pipe. I stopped briefly and exhaled the cloud on his approach toward me to give him a kiss. He allowed me to show him how much I had missed him in the bathroom of Charlie's apartment. It was during this sexual encounter I asked him if he wanted to get high. He ignored my question and said he was going upstairs to see Hutch and would be right back He wasn't gone longer than ten minutes. He returned, looked me straight in the eye and said " Zoe I am finished with getting high!" He didn't add and so are you. He said it with a seriousness I had never heard in his voice before. His eyes maintained contact with mine and I responded with "ok." Ernest said he had to check in with his Parole Officer within 48 hours. He informed me he would be going into a shelter as instructed by his Parole Officer. Then he gave me some money and said he would be back in the morning. I cooked Thanksgiving dinner and Earnest, Charlie and I enjoyed it together.

Poetic Recovery

However, with Earnest not getting high anymore I couldn't for the life of me find anything to be thankful for. Earnest came by everyday to see Charlie and I. He would give me money if he had any and of course I would give him some if I had it. Earnest was waiting to receive his social security benefits which were going to be substantial. What he did that amazed me, was he kept his word to himself and never used another illicit drug or drank alcohol again. It was during this time I would question Ernest how he could sit and watch me smoke cracks and not have the urge to join me. He said "during my last prison stay I learned that the joke is over and smoking crack just isn't fun anymore". He went on to say "I am too old to go back to prison and I don't want to die in prison alone." All that came out of my mouth was I sure hope God can work it out for me, as simply as he seems to have worked it out for you. My madness continued and I also kept selling drugs for my sister. Other dealers who thought my services would help their drug sales didn't hesitate to enlist my services. My disease of addiction led me to believe, if I changed my clothes on the hour the police wouldn't recognize me. I had a job to do and so did the police they did theirs better.

Life Don't Rhyme

Chapter Forty Six

On April 4th 1999 at 10 am in my haste to get high I made a sale to someone I didn't know. I was arrested, and charged with possession and the sale of a controlled substance in a school zone. I already had another case pending where I had been released on my own recognizance. Strange how you can ask God for help with one thing and he gives you the help you truly need. I was convicted and sentenced to three -six years. I had never served a prison sentence in New York State. I pleaded guilty and informed my mother that I had finally been rescued. I welcomed the opportunity to get off of Riker's Island. My destination was Bedford Hills Correctional Facility for Women. It was a massive facility surrounded by tall fences of razor wire. As the bus rolled up the hill toward the facility I watched a crew of men and women chopping down trees in a wooded area making room for more prison units. Bedford Hills was the first of three correctional facilities where I would be a guest. Bedford was the reception area where every body cavity would be thoroughly searched for contraband. Next I would undergo a physical examination and issued my state greens. State greens are standard issued uniforms that are required to be worn daily by every inmate. I would reside in Bedford Hills for a brief period of time before being transported further north to a medium security facility.

SECURITY

THEY ARE CUTTING DOWN TREES
TO GIVE ME A BETTER VIEW OF WHERE
I CANNOT BE.
THREE ROWS OF BARB WIRE ATOP EVERY FENCE
DO THEY NOT KNOW MY LIFE IS NOT OVER,
IT HAS ONLY JUST COMMENCED.
SECURITY IN PRISON IS AN IMPORTANT JOB
TO PROTECT SOCIETY FROM THOSE WHO KILL,
RAPE, CHEAT AND ROB.
THE REAL PRISON IS,
THE PRISON OF YOUR MIND.
UPON COMING TO THIS REALIZATION
I REFUSED TO IMPRISON MY MIND
FOR ANOTHER MOMENT OF "MY TIME."
I RE-INTRODUCED MYSELF TO MYSELF
I WAS DESPERATELY TRYING TO REACQUAINT
ME WITH WHO I REMEMBERED I USE TO BE.
FREQUENTLY ASKING MYSELF "AM I PLEASED
TO MEET ME." MY ANSWER IS YES. I HAVE
MADE UP MY MIND TO USE THIS TIME
TO FIND THE BEST IN ME.
A MAGNIFICENT CREATION OF GOD
BEAUTIFUL, STRONG, STURDY,
AND ABLE TO WITHSTAND ANY ILL WIND
TO NURTURE, EDUCATE, AND
RE-CONSTRUCT
THE BEAUTY OF THE TREE IN ME.

Life Don't Rhyme

A number was attached to every outer garment of clothing I received. The color was a dark drab forest green. Little did I know back then, this would be the color of my first interviewing suit when I finally returned to the free world. I spent eight weeks in Bedford Hills getting acquainted with the rules and regulations of all the facilities where I would be doing time. I often wondered where many of my female acquaintances were while I was in the streets of New York. My curiosity was satisfied after seeing many of those women in every facility I was in. Confirmation that I had relinquished all of my rights as a human being came when I was being shackled. My feet and hands were chained and I was ordered to board a bus destined for another woman's correctional facility, Albion. This facility was nick named Albion the Far Beyond. The only population consisted of inmates and corrections officers. Those who occupied the facility were either there to correct or to be corrected.

    The ride from Bedford Hills to this God forsaken prison was close to ten hours. There were no comfortable moments during this transfer. Our minds were focused on who would assist who when the need arose to use the bathroom. My new address was only an hour away from what once was my childhood home in Rochester, New York. Thoughts of a possible visit from my daddy flooded my mind. I made a mental note to use the first stamped envelope I could get my hands on to notify him of my

Poetic Recovery

location. Our arrival at Albion was late at night, and lights were out with the exception of those being used by inmates who worked as the reception crew. I had been informed that new jacks were usually assigned jobs that required physical labor. That information led me to create a physical disability that would exclude me from working in the mess hall and outside. I became truly grateful to my parents for insisting I finish high school. Something as simple as a high school diploma had great bearing on what work detail I would be assigned. When my mind was not consumed with the clouds of crack cocaine, I was actually a very effective teacher. Although I had not taught anyone, anything other than how to pack a stem or cook cocaine in flavors in years, I knew I was capable of teaching women how to read and write. So I requested a job in the school, tutoring adult basic education. This assignment would allow me to keep my mind focused on how to survive this ordeal. Now, you must understand my best thinking as a crack head afforded me free room and board at my new address on Old State School Road. I was not about to think myself any deeper into incarceration. You could always go deeper, into a place known SHU (segregated housing unit) if you exhibited behaviors not conducive to a correctional facility. During an inmate's time in SHU they were labeled as loss of life. This meant no commissary, no phone calls. You were only entitled to your mail. I figured out the key to

Life Don't Rhyme

avoiding SHU was to keep my mouth shut and to do as I was told. This would be a challenge I would take on and master during my eight month stay in Albion. The winters were brutal; no winter in Rochester, New York could have prepared me for the bitter cold that ravaged this compound. The huge facility when covered with snow looked like a scene taken from the movie *The Shining*.

    Little did I know during this episode in my life God would be doing his work. He would assist me with becoming a better person. The creature that lived in the darkness as a crack head was going to make a sincere effort toward deliverance and redemption.

Poetic Recovery

Chapter Forty Seven

Daily life in Albion came with non stop drama. Many of the corrections officers were on power trips, the men, as well as the women. There was underlined racism that reared its ugly head anytime an officer felt that you were trying to be insubordinate. There were countless accusations against correctional officers surrounding physical and sexual assaults upon the women daily. I recall passing a pool of blood that had run into the snow while going to breakfast one morning. A young woman had been savagely beaten by several guards for allegedly running off at the mouth. At that moment keeping my mouth shut was not an opition. My ability to write prompted me to begin getting signed statements from those women who witnessed the incident. Involving myself placed my safety at risk however, it was my responsibility to make sure that such an incident was never repeated. More importantly I recognized that this could be the recipe for another Attica. It was my responsibility to make sure this assault did not go unnoticed by those in power. It was my relationship with a fellow inmate Ellis that awakened the compassion within me to extend my help and my voice to another human being who was being violated. Soon after this incident I was visited by some investigators from the inmate's grievance committee who assured me no one would be privy to the information I had given them regarding the attack. I learned that compassion for your fellow man or woman has no place in the prison system; but if not here where? Women who lost loved ones were given the choice of a visit before death or attending the funeral. There are no exceptions to this in-humane practice. I knew from the moment I had to console a mother who had lost her child to the violence of the streets that I would never return to another correctional facility for as long as I was given the blessing of life. I couldn't help but put myself in this woman's position. I rocked her in my arms as she trembled and screamed tears of pain that only a mother could feel. This incident reminded me of the pain my addiction had caused the people who truly loved me. I learned there is no excuse for destroying your life. The many traumatic experiences I had survived in my life had not hardened my heart. For the first time in 29 years I allowed my humanity to show and shared the pain of another human being.

    The program committee made a decision to place me in a drug treatment program, ASAP (alcohol and substance abuse program). The program housed 40 women. We were all eligible for work release should we successfully complete this program without incident. ASAP was helpful and allowed me to begin putting some structure into my life. This structure consisted of simple tasks, such as getting up on

Poetic Recovery

time, preparing for the next day and organizing my surroundings to suit the following day's events. It is because I am prone to express myself best with pen and paper I began writng a feelings journal. I began writing my feelings surrounding daily events. These feelings developed into poems, skits, and short stories and gospel lyrics. I found a sense of release through writing my feelings on paper. I took on the responsibility of organizing the daily morning meetings that took place Monday through Friday before the regularly scheduled addiction workshops and groups. I read daily from my journal to my peers, whom I soon learned anticipated what I was going to do next. I finally tapped into the gut wrenching personal issues that plagued my existence from childhood. I learned I was by no means alone. I also learned that many women had endured similar trauma and abuse. The common denominators between me and these women was pain, suffering and we all ended up in the same place. More importantly we were all in need of corrections. I began participating in the therapeutic groups and activities that focused on my recreating me. ASAP had strict cardinal rules not unlike those of residential treatment facilities worldwide. Those rules included no sexual acting out, no physical violence or threats of physical violence. Should any of these rules be broken the consequences were SHU and the termination of your program. This would also eliminate you from work release consideration. I became what could be described as a model prisoner. This left me open to ridicule from many of my peers who were on the fence concerning positive change. I believed, since I was sincere and driven toward making positive changes in my attitude and behaviors, these same changes would spill over into my life. However, faith without works is dead. I also believed that for change to work I needed to become totally honest with myself concerning just how sick my addiction had made me. I took to writing my Daddy weekly, begging him to come and visit me. I had been such a grimy daughter. I didn't blame him in the least for not writing or visiting me. He had placed me on a pedestal and my drug use caused me to fall from grace in record breaking time, if I may add. Where my Daddy was concerned there was nothing he could do that would cause me to be angry with him. All my life I had been told that I was very much like him in so far as being my own person and headstrong. My brother Kenan was familiar with the horrors of addiction. He and his wife became a major source of support throughout this prison sentence. My mother always wrote to me and kept me abreast of weddings, funerals, and births that took place in my family. For the most part I always kept an open line of communication with my family members, whether they wrote back or not. It was during this time I accepted full responsibility for teaching my family how to treat

Poetic Recovery

the sub-human I had become. I told my loved ones except for my Daddy not to visit me. I accepted that I had created this situation and that there was no reason why my family should have to do this prison sentence with me. I learned there were jobs that I could perform for some of the inmates who couldn't read or write. These jobs would afford me the things I needed in commissary and could not afford to purchase myself. I was in demand to write letters for many of the women. I wrote to judges, foster parents, children, relatives, churches and Parole Boards. I learned how blessed I was to have parents who placed emphasis on learning and staying in school. Just the thought of having to work in the mess hall causes me severe discomfort. I met many women, who had been returned to Albion from the minimum security correctional facility, Taconic. They informed me they had been participants in another drug program, CASAT. (Comprehensive Alcohol Substance Abuse Treatment). They described it as being very strict and much more structured than my current program ASAP. I inquired why they had returned to Albion. What they told me next peaked my interest. They told me there was a male counselor there who didn't take any mess from women who were not there to commit themselves to saving their lives. Hearing about this man and the way these women spoke of his unorthodox methods of drug treatment made me determined to get through whatever was necessary in an effort to save my life. I knew I wanted to learn how to stay clean and I knew long before arriving in Taconic that this man would be the counselor to teach me. Many of the women who returned to Albion had violated the rules of the program. Some of them were honest about not wanting to stop using drugs. I understood perfectly that if you are not willing to change, all the tools and information will not keep you clean and sober. Believing that you are worthy of a life that doesn't include drugs, is difficult if your beginnings began in the addiction of a parent who is also trapped. The disease of addiction is an equal opportunity employer. Recovery is not impossible no matter what circumstances you have had to endure. What is necessary is that you must want recovery. Needing it will not be enough. I realized that developing a healthy relationship with myself was going to require total honesty from me. I had to address all the areas that contributed to my active addiction.

Poetic Recovery

Birth

I give birth to the words I write

I nurture them in serious thought

I arrange them with tender loving care

At first the thoughts are not very clear

So with pen and paper

I sit down and stare at the stark white walls

Sure enough my thoughts make a call

To the words I would like to say

As I put pen to paper

I begin writing words clear as day

The thoughts evolve into words

On paper they begin to take shape

The words, my babies start to grow

They grow into songs, short stories, and poems

One word after another they just seem to get along

Life Don't Rhyme

The one thing they do that makes me feel proud

They allow me to share my thoughts and
feelings with others out loud

The response I receive confirms my belief

My words give birth to all that breathe

Poetic Recovery

Chapter Forty Eight

It didn't concern me that this counselor ran a strict unit. I knew drug dealers that ran strict sales operations and often the only bonus you received was jail or death. Anticipating that there was someone in the world who could assist me with getting my life back gave me the hope I needed to endure anything. I began volunteering for any and every thing having to do with my recovery. Yeah, I had an ulterior motive for volunteering for projects; which was getting a transfer to Taconic. Volunteering would place me in position to be granted CASAT (comprehensive alcohol substance abuse treatment) program. I had to not only complete the ASAP program I had to live it, breath it, speak it, and more importantly walk it. I facilitated groups, ran morning meetings, and wrote skits. These skits were performed by the women. The skits were about being able to recognize triggers that could contribute to a potential relapse. I would write gospel lyrics and create melodies to perform during morning meeting. These activities provided me with the points I needed to leave Albion and increase my chances of being sent down state to the Taconic Correctional Facility for Women. I learned during my time in Albion, that I was capable of doing more with my life other than smoking crack cocaine. I recall telling my mother that it would be a great investment for her pay into a life insurance policy for me. I said this believing my life would go up in the smoke my lungs consumed daily through the stem of the crack pipe. I learned that women are to be celebrated daily for being the teachers and givers of life. The time came for my case to be reviewed for the transfer to Taconic, I was approved and for that I was grateful. I began getting on my knees daily to pray for the strength and patience to endure the change that I believed I wanted and knew I needed. When I arrived at Taconic I learned there was the six month waiting list to get into the CASAT (comprehensive alcohol substance abuse treatment) program. During this time I had to be assigned a job function. Once again, I had to convince another program committee that I wasn't capable of performing physical labor. (This is the behavior of an addict contemplating recovery, ie:manipulation for the sole purpose of avoiding unnecessary exhaustion). Of course the job functions they needed to fill were in the yard and the mess hall; not at all what I had in mind. I needed to make some connections quickly before I was placed in a work assignment where I would actually have to work. Wouldn't you know it? Here comes God again to the rescue. I was assigned to my living quarters and my cell mate informed me that she worked as a tutor and was changing jobs. She knew the teacher needed a replacement and arranged for an introduction with the teacher, Mrs. Lunnigan.

Poetic Recovery

She was a nice woman who was dedicated to teaching women adult basic education. Many were completely illiterate and some were just not willing to improve their quality of life. I received the work assignment because she specifically requested me. This job assignment allowed me time to write more poetry and gospel lyrics. More importantly, it revealed a sense of gratitude I had for the many people in my life that loved me and taught me the importance of becoming an intelligent woman. So many women I met were alone with no support or source of encouragement on the outside. I worked hard to help those women with whom I came in contact. I enjoyed assisting them with their studies. I felt useful and productive knowing I was helping these women to boost their self esteem in addition to motivating them to want to improve their quality of life. Change is uncomfortable if you have been conditioned to believe that you are not worthy of anymore than what is handed to you. Many women in prison are without outside support networks that inspire, and encourage change while incarcerated. It is because of this fact that women must uplift, inspire and encourage each other.

Life Don't Rhyme

Oh Well

What is the purpose of someone who writes?

It certainly should be to give others insight

To enable people to be aware, to want to care

To see other places, they could be

To give encouragement and spread information

Is writing not a creative form of communication?

So when I allow other to know what it is I feel

I do not lie

I write the truth of what I believe to be real

If there are those who choose not to read or listen

Oh Well

I take pleasure in knowing what I say has been written

Poetic Recovery

Suddenly another opportunity presented itself. Two female professors volunteered to teach a creative writing course combined with an English 101 college course one night a week. I enrolled the moment registrations were being accepted. I was thrilled to learn I had been accepted. Ms. Gina Shea and Ms. Della Corte offered English 101 classes to those inmates with high school diplomas or GED's who were interested in attaining college credit. Well, I jumped on it. It didn't interfere with my job function and it offered me the audience I needed to convince myself that my writing could be taken seriously. We were given assignments to be completed on time just as would be expected in a college setting. Our professors were dedicated to encouraging the women they worked with. They gave us the motivation and encouragement needed to believe we were capable of achieving academic success. It was their dedication that would serve to change the minds of many women who believed their existence did not matter to the world. Though I truly enjoyed my class my focus was doing whatever it took to get home. In this particular instance what it took, was for me to do what I loved, and I genuinely loved to write. The class was small, to ensure that each student would receive the individual attention they required. Camaraderie was established among the women who participated. We conversed with each other about our assignments and topics that concerned us daily.

Life Don't Rhyme

We discussed, and debated different interpretations of required readings. We held each other's confidence sacred, while offering constructive criticism. We respected each other's opinions, and the right to voice them. We allowed ourselves to venture outside of our circumstances and explore the possibilities. The residue of my drug use was clearing. I was finding some clarity and purpose for my life on earth. Though I still struggled with taking shortcuts daily, I would check myself. Taking shortcuts in my life had caused me to miss out on living a good life for 29 years. So I began to focus on changing my sick thinking. This would require commitment and becoming open to constructive criticism and correction in the world of drug treatment this is known as a pull-up.

Poetic Recovery

SOMETHING TO SAY

SOMEONE ONCE TOLD ME I COULD WRITE
I KNEW I WOULD NOT BECOME A SUCCESS OVER NIGHT
AS I BEGAN TO WRITE
THE WINDOWS OF MY MIND OPENED EXTREMELY WIDE
THE MORE I WROTE THE MORE I SAW
SUDDENLY WHAT HAD BEEN FROZEN BEGAN TO THAW
AS THE MYSTERIES OF MY LIFE SLOWLY REVEALED
IF I CONTINUED TO WRITE
I WOULD CONTINUE TO HEAL
THOUGH BEING HURT IN LIFE IS SAID TO HELP US GROW
BELIEVE ME WHEN I SAY MY HEART IS SORE
THE WORDS I WRITE ARE THE WORDS THAT FREE
ALL I FEEL INSIDE OF ME
SATISFACTION IS MY GREATEST JOY
IT FILLS ME RICHLY LIKE DOM PERIGNON AND BELUGA CAVIAR
THE THRILL OF WRITING FOR ME
IS WHEN PEOPLE READ AND LISTEN WITH THEIR HEARTS TO EVERY WORD
SATISFACTION ARRIVES KNOWING MY WORK HAS BEEN FAVORABLY RECIEVED
I AND GOD BOTH KNOW BEFORE I MAKE IT INTO PRINT MUCH OF MY WORK WILL BE REJECTED
RECOGNITION WILL BE WHAT WILL SWEEP ME OFF MY FEET AND STEAL MY HEART AWAY
BECAUSE IT WILL CONFIRM I DEFINITELY HAVE SOMETHING TO SAY

Life Don't Rhyme

Chapter Forty Nine

The first assignment was to write a piece that would allow my professors to know us as people. We were informed that we would be called upon to read our assignments aloud. I was excited about being able to share my work with women who were genuinely interested in assisting me with developing my craft. I was equally excited about hearing the thoughts of my peers. Each woman was gifted in her own form of expression. Though this class was held one time weekly for two hours, all of my peers anticipated it as if it were the premier of a feature film. Like any writer, I lost myself in the creation of my work. I found confinement to be a welcomed luxury toward helping me develop my work. I welcomed count time when the entire population of the prison was counted one by one. This is a security measure utilized by the department of corrections nationwide. I was guaranteed at least 45 minutes, four times daily to devote to my assignments. My journal and poetry consumed my every waking moment. I would write wherever and whenever a thought captured my mind. My memories offered me the vivid pictures I required to paint many pages with words. The following is the results of my first assignment. I would write wherever and whenever a thought captured my mind. Words would be my life line out of prison. The following is the results of my first assignment.

Poetic Recovery

Memory is A Jewel

While daydreaming surrounded by the cardinal elements
Memories rush in like tides from the ocean
To the shores of the black sandy beaches of my mind
How I long to wrap my body loosely
In rich earth tone colors of chiffon
Linking me to the freedom I have lost
I recall the brilliant rays of sunlight
reflecting what appear to be diamonds
beneath my feet
Feet that are now shackled
No more freedom do they seek
Memories are the only link to freedom that will always keep me free
Without these precious jewels only God knows where I'd be
So I continue to free the treasures of my mind
As I continue to daydream while doing time

Life Don't Rhyme

This piece of work drew the interest of my professors and they encouraged me to continue to write. I wrote with the ferocity of someone who had been given less than a year to live. I found with each poem I wrote I freed myself from a piece of my past that contributed to my disease of addiction. It would be my CASAT counselor Mr. Major, Ms Shea, and Ms. Della Corte who would become my major sources of encouragement. They demanded that I dig deeper within myself in order to find closure with those issues that had damaged my life. They requested that I share those situations with women who also shared the same pain.

Writing allowed me to peel away what I believe were twenty nine layers of guilt and shame. One layer for each year I allowed crack cocaine to own me. It was told to me, if an addict is not working on something, something was surely working on them. So work I did! Every free moment was devoted to my studies and more importantly to re-creating me.

Poetic Recovery

Chapter Fifty

     I was still on the waiting list for CASAT and writing allowed me the luxury of not focusing on time. Finally the day arrived and I was notified my wait for the CASAT program had come to an end. I was instructed to pack my property as I would be moving into a new building to attend the CASAT program. As I walked into the building I was informed I would be going to K gallery. The moment I realized that the male counselor I had heard so much about was located on J gallery I immediately went to work on a scheme to get transferred to his floor.(there's that shortcut behavior I was talking about) After conducting a full scale investigation of K gallery's current CASAT counselor I learned the only knowledge she possessed about addiction was what she read and learned from books. I was convinced the only thing she could possibly teach me would be how to get up and go to work every day. Don't misunderstand; this was a feat I had not achieved in my entire life thus far. I certainly couldn't include selling or smoking cracks as an employable skill. However, it was full time job, and public relations skills were mandatory. I knew I desperately wanted someone who knew about the deeply rooted issues that started the ball of addiction rolling over and through the lives of people like myself. Well, they say "be careful what you ask for, because you just might get it," I did. One

Life Don't Rhyme

particular day all the women of K gallery were informed that our counselor was unable to get to work. We were instructed that our addiction workshop would take place on J gallery. Mr. Major would be taking over for the day. I was excited as this would be the first time I would get to see this counselor Mr. Major in action. The group was in a circle and the women of K gallery were instructed by a peer aide to join the circle. Each woman received a handout entitled "I am your disease." This handout covered all of the chaos the disease of addiction had caused in our lives. Before the group began a tall, chocolate brown, bald man entered the room. He stopped and stood perfectly still. His gentle eyes scanned the entire group, looking at each woman. It was a no-nonsense kind of look. He was dressed in brown corduroy slacks, a burnt orange turtle neck sweater topped with a mustard colored suede blazer. His shoes appeared to be soft brown suede. My toothless mouth dropped open when he introduced himself as Mr. Major the CASAT counselor of J Gallery. From that moment every woman was silent. We were not given the option of volunteering to read. Mr. Major made his own selection. The purpose of this exercise was to evoke honesty as to who would acknowledge that the content of the handout was in fact that woman's disease of addiction. My first thought of what I was witnessing was some corny charade the women were participating in so they would be granted work release. I was greatly mistaken and happily relieved to know I was absolutely wrong. Here was a black man who's only goal was to assure each woman that she was worthy of a life that would allow her to live more, be more and do more. Unbelievable! You must understand that it takes a special man to work with females, especially women in prison. The majority of these women are desperately searching for acceptance and love. Mr. Major made it clear that he was going to love us all until we were able to love ourselves. He took on the role of a highly respected and sometimes feared father figure. He followed every rule and taught each woman the importance of following those same rules. He restored self respect, integrity and dignity. I was called upon to read from the handout and Mr. Major instructed me to read it as though I were angry with my disease of addiction. I did as I was told and by the time I finished reading I was in complete tears. I actually felt the devastation my drug use had inflicted on my life and the lives of my family members. Knowing that Mr. Major was the only male CASAT counselor I wrote a letter to the department head of the CASAT program. I informed him that I had an issue with female counselors, and based on my criminal history it would be advantageous to my recovery if I were transferred to a male counselor. God was truly looking out for me and the lie I told, because the next day I was given permission to attend

Life Don't Rhyme

groups in J gallery until a bed became available. Women in prison are just as caddy and petty as they are on the street, J gallery was no different. I was already acquainted with many of the women as a result of drug use and other stays in various correctional facilities. As women of J-gallery we were required to set standards for ourselves and demonstrate role model behavior at all times. Mr. Major took each woman's transformation seriously. It was common knowledge among the corrections officers in the facility that if any woman from J-gallery was involved in any negative behavior she would be held accountable. She would also be confronted by her peers in what is known as encounter group. Mr. Major had no problem assuring every woman that, though he may be disappointed in negative behavior he still loved us. He made it his personal responsibility to make sure a learning experience was assigned to every women involved in any form of negative behavior. That assignment would cause a woman to think of the many consequences of negative behavior. In prison they could lead to SHU, her dismissal from the CASAT program and her eligibility for work release. In society negative behaviors could result in a return trip to prison, or a final trip to death. It was not until I attended the CASAC program that I considered the consquences of anything. As an active addict I thought of my consequences as being the result of my life style not having anything to do

Poetic Recovery

with my decision making. I learned how impulsive behavior plays a role in the outcome of any and all situations. In the days that followed I thanked God for giving me a counselor that I believed in and who believed in me. I knew Mr. Major could help me learn how to live life on life's terms. He placed in a position where I could get honest with myself, and ultimately forgive myself for all the hurt and pain I allowed my active addiction to inflict in my life.

Life Don't Rhyme

J Gallery

Together we stand, divided we fall
Why do you riff when I say clear the hall
You have created feelings of anger in me
Instead of confronting me, you spread your misery
Are we not our brothers and sisters keepers
There are times when it's hard to tell
You say "I can't be bothered with you
I'm living in my own hell"
The changes I took myself through in the street, have re-arrested my mind in prison.
It's gotten to the point where I can't sleep.
Is this not enough torment to contemplate change?
If nothing changes, nothing changes.
On the count, On the chow, On the program
Have you not yet realized who is in command?
I look at you and see myself another addict
To damn cool to ask for help
Just take a moment, look around and see
The hands reaching out to help you
Stand in recovery.
Erase the image you are unable to maintain
I can tell you with that false image you have nothing to gain.
Learning the significance of structure is essential to life
Recovery is not the enemy,
Recovery is Life!

Poetic Recovery

Chapter Fifty One

As I reflect back on my first learning experience I understand why I and my peers wanted to nominate Mr. Major for sainthood. He gave us hope! The man told me that in order for this program to work, I had to become open, honest, and willing. It was easier said than done. I began making a half ass attempt, and became frustrated with having to change my way of thinking. He explained to me that my drug use had tainted my rational thought process. He went on to explain that if I didn't change, it would inevitably lead me back to using crack cocaine or worse. Being in treatment meant you could not condone the wrong doings or negative behaviors of another peer. More importantly you had to grow in this process or face a learning experience. Non compliance would certainly get you sent back to Albion. A contract was a learning experience that allowed you to perform a task of physical labor, cleaning bathrooms, showers, mopping and sweeping floors, combined with written assignments. Growth always included telling on your peers as well as yourself. I received one contract during my stay on J-Gallery. I condoned and conspired to allow the negative behaviors of two women to go un-confronted. My actual role was passing letters for a lesbian couple Netty and Ne Ne who were on a speaking ban. The moment I was confronted the first thing that came out of my mouth was "I'm leaving this corny ass shit." It was at that moment Mr. Major took me into his office and offered me an opportunity to set an example for the other women who also thought the program was corny. He also demanded I take ownership for the role I played in condoning the negative behaviors of my peers. He explained to me that by complying with the contract I accepted responsibility for my actions. He told me I would be saving the lives of other women who needed the program. I questioned him as to why he believed I could influence the other women who desperately needed treatment. He sat in silence for a moment before answering me. Mr. Major confirmed for me what I had known all the time; that I had a gift to influence people. He explained that during my active addiction I used the gift to continue getting high. He told me I could flip the script and use my ability to influence others to help those who needed it. What touched my heart was when he said "I understand that you don't love yourself right now, but allow me to love you until you can love yourself." He was passionate about saving the lives of the women who were entrusted to him. It was that very day I surrendered to my disease of addiction and all the negative behaviors I had acquired as a result of my drug use. I did my contract like a champ. I spoke daily in groups, volunteered for job functions, and became a peer aide. This time I was indeed ready to let go and let God. More importantly I

Poetic Recovery

was ready to turn it over to a power greater than myself. This change did not come over me all at once. I still struggle in many areas because I continue to be a work in progress. The blessing is I don't debate with what is right and wrong. I work full time at getting out of my own way.

I recall the pain and suffering resulting from my not having a power greater than myself in my life. There are many little sayings that come to mind when I am wrestling with an issue. The one that always leads me to where I want to be is "Do the right thing even when no one is looking." I learned that change is difficult. I learned the ability to ask for help will assist me in making a smooth transition from the valley's of my life to the mountain tops.

Change is totally uncomfortable, which is why I surrendered. I knew by changing now I could alleviate severe discomfort up the road. I had already been down the road and it led to disaster, so the only direction to go is up.

Life Don't Rhyme

TURN IT OVER

THERE WAS A TIME IN MY LIFE WHEN PEOPLE
CALLED ME TIO SHORT FOR TURN IT OVER
I BELIEVED MYSELF TO BE
A HUSTLER IN EVERY SENSE OF THE WORD
WHEN ANYONE SPOKE
MONEY IS ALL I HEARD
I STARTED OUT SELLING ONE BUNDLE OF
DOPE
BREAK IT DOWN INTO TWO DO IT AGAIN AND
REGROUP.
THEN I FLIPPED TWO INTO FOUR
AND FOUR INTO EIGHT
BEFORE I KNEW IT I WAS STRAIGHT
AND THE CASH FLOW WAS GREAT
MY WORKERS NEVER ENTERTAINED
ANY THOUGHTS OF TELLING ME
SOME OKEY DOKE.
THEY KNEW IF MY MONEY WASN'T RIGHT
I WOULD CUT THEIR THROATS
NOW I HAD A LONG RUN, MADE PLENTY
MONEY, AND CARRIED A GUN.
SURE I SHED SOME BLOOD ALONG THE WAY
THAT COMES WITH THE TERRITORY
IF YOU WANT TO GET PAID
BUT WITH HUSTLING COMES THE POLICE
TO PROTECT WHAT IS MINE
I HAVE TO KEEP MY PIECE
BUT HUSTLING GOT HECTIC
MY ENEMIES GOT RELEASED
BEFORE I KNEW IT
THE BODY COUNT INCREASED

Poetic Recovery

I BEGAN TO FEEL TRAPPED
NO ONE TO WATCH MY BACK
WHEN THE SNITCHES CAME OUT
I KNEW I HAD TO RUN
HUSTLING HAD JUST STOPPED BEING FUN
NOW I LIVE MY LIFE ON THE RUN
WHAT I USE TO SELL FOR MONEY
HAS BECOME MY FUN
BEING ON THE LAM, IT'S HARD TO STAY HIGH
THE LAST HUSTLER I ROBBED
SAID I WOULD DIE
WHEN I'M SICK
IT DOES NOT MATTER WHO I KNOCK
AS LONG AS I GET MY FIX AND MY ROCK
BUT THE LAST STICKUP DIDN'T GO SO HOT
I'M LAID UP IN THE HOSPITAL
BECAUSE I GOT SHOT
AS I OPENED MY MOUTH TO TALK
THE DOCTOR SAID YOU WILL NEVER WALK
AS THE TEARS BEGAN TO FALL FROM MY EYES
I BEGGED THE LORD TO PLEASE LET ME DIE
YET I LIVED TO TELL THIS STORY
YES, PEOPLE STILL CALL ME TIO
THOUGH THE NICKNAME IS THE SAME
THE PERSON HAS BEEN CHANGED
I AM LYING HERE PARALYZED
FROM THE WAIST DOWN
ALONE IN THIS ROOM
UNABLE TO HEAR A SOUND
AS MY EYES BECOME ACCUSTOMED TO THE GLOOM I KNOW NOW I WAS NEVER REALLY ALONE IN THAT ROOM

Life Don't Rhyme

THE WORDS TURN IT OVER
PLAY OVER AND OVER IN MY HEAD
TURN IT OVER TURN IT OVER
YOU KNOW YOU COULD BE DEAD
TURN IT OVER TURN IT OVER
DON'T BE AFRAID
I AM THE LORD YOUR GOD
I ALONE CAN HEAL YOUR PAIN
YES I WANTED TO BE HEALED
THOUGH SOMETHING DEEP INSIDE WAS
STILL
SEARCHING FOR A DEAL
I HAD BECOME SO COMFORTABLE IN MY SIN
I DID NOT KNOW WHAT WAS REAL
THEN I HEARD MYSELF SCREAMING
GOD HELP ME PLEASE
I FELL FROM THE BED TO THE FLOOR
STRUGGLING TO RAISE UP ON MY KNEES
HERE IS WHAT I SAID
AS I CONTINUED TO BEG
GOD YOU SAY YOU LOVE ME, WHY?
I DON'T UNDERSTAND IT
I HAVE BROKEN ALL OF YOUR
COMMANDMENTS
YET YOU STILL ALLOW ME TO LIVE
AFTER ALL I HAVE DONE
AND IT HAS TAKEN FOR ME NOT TO WALK
TO SAY YOU HAVE WON
IT TOOK FOR THIS TO HAPPEN TO ME
TO BE DELIVERED AND REDEEMED
FOR I CAN CLEARLY SEE THE WINNER IS NOT
YOU THE WINNER IS ME.

Chapter Fifty Two

Mr. Major strongly suggested that once a woman completed the CASAT program she should fortify her tools by going into a six month residential work release program in Phoenix House located in Brooklyn. More treatment was not something I anticipated. However I gave it considerable thought after reading letters from women who were former inmates and participants of CASAT on J-gallery. They kept us informed of how they were doing. The women who successfully completed treatment in J-gallery wrote letters about everything we needed to know before returning to society. These letters had great information and often pictures of the Phoenix House where I would hopefully be living once I successfully completed the CASAT program. For the most part people in general always need to be reassured about situations they are powerless over and I was no different. I didn't want to walk into any environment blind. (imagine trust issues from someone who stuck her money in a hole and prayed for a real crack to come out) This powerlessness thing was new to me. Trusting in the accuracy of other's description of Phoenix House was scary at best. Having always been blunt and straight forward with what is on my mind I have come to expect the same of others. Truth is to be served straight up without a chaser enabling one to feel the full impact.

Life Don't Rhyme

SUGAR COATED

WHY WOULD YOU SUGAR COAT RECOVERY ?
YOU DIDN'T BUY SUGAR COATED DOPE.
YOU DIDN'T BUY SUGAR COATED COKE.
SO DON'T ENTER INTO RECOVERY AS A JOKE
BELIEVING IF YOU MEMORIZE THE 12 STEPS
THEY WILL KEEP YOU AFLOAT.
REALIZE WHEN SAYING THE SERENITY
PRAYER
THE ONLY WAY TO RECOVER IS TO KEEP
YOUR HIGHER POWER NEAR.
SO WHY SUGAR COAT RECOVERY?
DID YOU NOT BUY THE BEST NARCOTICS
RAW?
SO DO YOU NOT REQUIRE THE SAME PURITY
IN YOUR RECOVERY BY LAW?
WITHOUT THAT DISCOVERY, YOU WILL
NEVER FIND PURE AND SIMPLE RECOVERY.
RECOVERY CAN TAKE YOU TO NEW AND
SOBER HIGHS, WHERE ADDICTION KEPT YOU
FROM BEFORE.
THROUGH RECOVERY YOU WILL BE ABLE TO
UNLOCK ANY AND EVERY DOOR.
BUT DON'T BE MISGUIDED BY THE HYPE
TO SUGAR COAT RECOVERY IS TO SUGAR
COAT LIFE.
KEEP IT SIMPLE, KEEP IT RAW
BY DOING THIS YOU CAN REST ASSURE
STRAIGHT UP RECOVERY IS NOT A CURE
IT IS A MEANS TO TAKE MY LIFE BACK
FROM THE ADDICT WHO IS ME.

Poetic Recovery

I continued to attend my English 101 class one evening a week. However, my writing took on a new focus, recovery. I wrote about my recovery daily just as I wrote about my past. This writing helped me to internalize the information I had been given in order to do whatever was necessary to keep from returning to active addiction and prison. It allowed me to focus on where I was going in my life. I completed my English class and enrolled again for a second cycle. I continued to progress in my treatment and I began to recognize small changes in the way I thought primarily the way I viewed right and wrong. I learned it was deadly for me to rationalize the two. During my active addiction I rationalized daily and the outcome was always disastrous. In treatment I learned to keep things simple in black and white leaving no room for me to paint a grey area. I encouraged the women who came into treatment with the attitude of just wanting to do their time toward doing something different and not to leave the same way they arrived. I encouraged them to take advantage of this gift called recovery. For those peers who utilized the prison system as a seasonal vacation home my words of encouragement fell on deaf ears. There were many who wanted to be encouraged and reassured that there is life after addiction. I did my best to "walk the walk." Just being able to talk the talk is not enough to an addict who is new to the recovery process because it would sound like *game*. I did my best to incorporate one hundred percent change into my life keeping in mind that being human, perfection is not an option. I would have to acknowledge and embrace my shortcomings in order to get better. I felt confident in having made the decision to go into treatment at Phoenix House upon my completion of the CASAT program and my release from prison. When the time came I was informed that there was yet another waiting list for Phoenix House. I was told once again that until a bed became available I would have to be housed in another women's correctional facility, Bayview. It was located on the West Side Highway and 20th Street in Manhattan. The area was a trap, because it turned into ho stroll at night. I immediately put my pen and paper into action. I requested the warden allow me to remain in Taconic on J-gallery until a bed became available in Phoenix House. I explained to her an interruption in my treatment would not be conducive to my recovery and the hard work I had put in toward becoming a better person, would be threatened in such an environment. Wouldn't you know it, God came through and permitted me to remain in the care of Mr. Major until a bed opened up in Phoenix House. My peers called me insane and crazy, I ignored them. What was important to me was to know that no corrections officer would ever call me on the count, on the chow or on the gate. I was scared and had been with me long enough to know that I was good at acting as

Poetic Recovery

though I had it all together. What I learned was that my addiction was not an act where the curtain would close after each scene. It was alive and well and I needed to safeguard my life if I ever expected to have a life. I learned to tell on my disease when it talked to me about what kind of crack we were going to smoke when I was released. I knew my ability to tell on my disease would save my life. Mr. Major told us that he had given each woman a flashlight and a map that we should follow to the letter. Under no circumstances were we to deviate from that map. I made my mind up to take the suggestions that were given and to stay out of my head alone. Thinking on my own was still dangerous. I accepted the fact I needed help and would not let my ego prevent me from asking for it. During those three additional months my writing became an obsession that allowed me to expand my thought process. I created new gospel lyrics that I sang during the prison church services. The poetry I created flowed from deep within. I reviewed many of the lesson plans, I had been taught since coming into the CASAT program. I kept detailed notes of every lesson plan Mr. Major created. The one lesson plan I referred to most often was that of powerlessness. It was tough accepting powerlessness, until I discovered by accepting powerlessness only then would I have power.

Life Don't Rhyme

Chapter Fifty Three

In January 2001 I was notified a bed had become available and that I would depart from Taconic Correctional Facility to go to Phoenix House on January 17th 2001. The first thing that came to mind was, what shall I wear? I had worn forest green for close to 24 months. The moment I was given the freedom to choose what I wanted to wear it dawned on me that I didn't own any clothing that didn't have my state numbers embossed on them. I called my mother whose constant faith and prayers helped to deliver me from the darkness of addiction. She happily sent me a couple of outfits to wear and none of them were green! Though I was still conscious of my appearance, I knew that my permanent wardrobe was the armor of my higher power, designed by grace and mercy. My daily accessories were sobriety, strength, a map and a flashlight that would guide me throughout my life in recovery. Words can't describe the feeling of being driven in a vehicle, yet alone a car without shackles. I knew I did not want to return to the sounds of gates closing, and correctional officers screaming "on the chow" and "on the count." I told myself during that ride to Brooklyn that I was going to make my time count for something. I was taking my birthright back. Mr. Major told everyone that by being in a correctional facility we had handed over our birthright to live happy, joyous and

Poetic Recovery

free, over to the corrections officers the moment we made the decision to use illicit drugs and commit a crime. We volunteered to allow others to correct our lives. Mr. Major told me "living in recovery would enable me to live more, do more, and be more" and that is just what I set out to do. I refused to become another statistic whose life is spent going in and out of the revolving doors of correctional facilities, where inmates and correction officers knew each other on a first name basis.

    I arrived at the Phoenix House treatment facility in Brooklyn with four other women. The facility wasn't a facility at all. It was a three story brownstone building that had recently been renovated to accommodate seventy five women comfortably. It was located on a beautiful tree lined street not far from downtown Brooklyn. There were no bars on any doors or windows, and I was happy I made the decision to come. I was informed during orientation that I would have to report to the Bay View facility to register as a resident of Phoenix House and a parolee the next day. After that I would not be allowed outside for thirty days. I really had no problem with the thirty day restriction having endured 24 months behind bars and razor wire fences. I was assigned a room with five other women. I was informed my duties as a peer aide in my CASAT program preceded me and that my work assignment would be on structure as the coordinator.

Life Don't Rhyme

Another blessing that came with my arrival to Phoenix House was a dynamic woman who was the new Deputy Director. She was appointed at a time when it was necessary to re-establish the true meaning and purpose of residential treatment. This woman was wealth of knowledge and compassion which she gave freely to both her staff and clients. She demanded the women of Phoenix house take steps to rise to our full potential so we would not have to return to prison. I am forever in her debt. I was assigned a counselor, Koryn. She was strict and demanded the truth about who I was and what I wanted to become. I really had not given much thought as to what type of career I was going to pursue. I did know I wanted to write, however the Parole required that I become gainfully employed as a stipulation of work release and a parolee. This fact confirmed I was still the property of New York State. I assumed the job function of coordinator in the program as seriously as if I were getting paid. I became quite good at scheduling and overseeing job functions performed by my peers. I was also a trusted escort for my peers without solo status.
I was greeted with much disfavor by my peers. I was always ridiculed for doing the right thing and labeled a TC (THERAPEUTIC COMMUNITY) Robot. I never missed an opportunity to confront my peers about their negative behaviors. I also commended them for the positive unselfish acts they demonstrated.

Poetic Recovery

Wherever and whenever women live together you are guaranteed continuous drama. Lying while in jail is a common practice of every inmate. They all consist of how everyone was somebody getting money when they were in the street. Every story is subject to change each time it is told by someone who is in deep denial. Women just like men have a need to be accepted among their peers. Both genders create lies while incarcerated, not giving a second thought as to whether or not they will ever see the person they have lied to again in life. These lies inevitably reveal frauds.

Life Don't Rhyme

FRAUDS

YOU CLAIM TO BE A WOMAN
SURELY YOU JEST

FROM THE TIME I AWAKE, UNTIL I GO TO SLEEP

THESE SO CALLED WOMEN CONTINUE TO BEEF

WHY DO YOU PERSIST IN CALLING YOURSELVES WOMEN?

THESE NON-DESCRIPT NO REASON FOR LIVING

LYING ASS, WANNA BE WOMEN

THEY SPREAD VICIOUS LIES AND SPEW VENOM

YET THEY STILL WANT TO BE ACKNOWLEDGED AS WOMEN.

HOW CAN THIS BE?

WHEN YOU WONT TAKE RESPONSIBILITY FOR WHAT YOU HAVE BECOME

THE DEPARTMENT OF CORRECTIONS HOLDS YOUR LIVES IN IT'S HANDS

Poetic Recovery

IT IS DURING THIS TIME THAT YOU MUST
COME TO UNDERSTAND

WOMEN, EACH OTHER IS ALL YOU HAVE

ENCOURAGE, TEACH, AND EMPOWER
EACH OTHER WITH KNOWLEDGE AND
INFORMATION THAT WILL ENHANCE YOUR
QUALITY OF LIFE

STOP VOLUNTEERING TO FILL UP THE
PRISONS AND THE JAILS
STOP LEAVING YOUR CHILDREN A LEGACY
TO FAIL

THE MAJORITY OF US WHO RESIDE BEHIND
BARS DO SO
BECAUSE WE WERE IN SEARCH OF
SOMETHING OR POSSIBLY SOMEONE TO
VALIDATE OUR EXISTENCE

LET THE SEARCH END NOW!

YOU ARE ROYALTY

NO ONE CAN VALIDATE THE CHILD OF A
KING

Life Don't Rhyme

ChapterFifty Four

While in Phoenix House I met with the job developer. He would assist me in acquiring full time employment with a minimum of thirty five hours. His resources left much to be desired. I finally met powerlessness face to face when I was scheduled for an interview with a fast food chain located in Rockefeller Center. I had been trying to outrun working in kitchens for the past two years only to end up in a burger joint. One can only imagine my disappointment. My first day was a disaster. I burned the hamburgers and while attempting to re-fill the ketchup containers, the ketchup went all over everything and everyone behind the counter. It was equivalent to a scene from an I Love Lucy episode. The second day they put me on the floor wiping and clearing off tables. I went back to the job developer at Phoenix House and told him I was not cut out for fast food service. I told him I needed a suit to interview for a proper job. He scheduled me for an interview with an organization known as Dress for Success. He told me that this organization was geared toward assisting women who wanted to re-enter the work force. He said they would suit me with the proper business attire to help a woman such as myself feel confident in her efforts to acquire gainful employment. I was excited at the thought of possibly having something new to wear. I didn't have any money other than my weekly stipend from Phoenix House and I needed all the help I could get. I kept my appointment with Dress for Success arriving early, ensuring that I would be on time. The woman who assisted me was gracious, attentive, helpful and non judgmental. She treated me as though I were a customer with money in one of the finer department stores. I found a suit that looked professional. The cut was tailored and flattering to a body that had put on some extra pounds. And would you believe it? It was green. You would think after wearing that color for so long I would have picked another color. I took the color of the suit as a warning sign. It would serve to remind me if I did not remain committed to my recovery and creating a better life it would only be a matter of time before I returned to prison wearing this same color green. I was given a choice of shoes and decided on a pair of low heeled green pumps. I was then given stockings, a purse, and some great Bobbi Brown makeup. At that moment I felt like a female superhero who was fully equipped to leap into the work force in a single bound. When leaving the offices of Dress for Success I was given information that would keep me connected to this organization and the great work they do for many years to come. I learned during my first visit at Dress for Success the volunteers and staff were genuinely concerned about my being able to become gainfully employed. The women of this organization are angels whose sole purpose is to lead every woman who docks in its doorway back to self sufficiency. I began a love affair with this organization from day one and it continues to this very day.

    The female work release program of Phoenix House was situated around many churches. The women had been given permission to attend one in particular, because they provided a chaperone. Brotherhood Baptist Church of Brooklyn served as a source of spiritual wealth and guidance to many of the woman who came through the work release program. Their clergy would come and pick us up each Sunday. They provided dinner after the service and called the staff of Phoenix House if a service was going to cause us to return to the facility late. The staff of Phoenix House encouraged its woman to find a source of spirituality that would help in strengthening their support network. I spent plenty of time developing a relationship with my higher power while incarcerated. Most inmates find religion in prison in order to get out of your cell to meet with someone else. Someone told me that if God ever seems far away, guess who moved? Today I stand still and remain faithful in my belief that the God I serve can do everything but fail!

Poetic Recovery

HEY BEAUTIFUL

How many times have I stared in the mirror
wondering who you are
Do you exist?
Are you actually here?
Are you near, or far?
From where I sit,
It appears to be much to late
To be rescued by a knight in shining armor
I have long since passed the stage where I needed to be saved
There are still moments when I do think about being in love with someone
A person who can love me who is not in love with drugs
Twenty-nine years is a long time to never love me
So, mystery lover if you do exist,
I am afraid you will have to take a number
And join the list
For you see, at this stage in my life to attempt to love someone else
When I am still struggling with
Whether or not I love myself
Just wouldn't be fair
I am learning to overcome the horrors I came from
I breathe them, taste them and feel them
I need is time to heal them
I have managed to get a grip
Continuing my journey through recovery
without a slip
And when time permits you may possibly find me
my love
I am the beauty who does not use drugs

Life Don't Rhyme

Chapter Fifty Four

The next day I went in search of another job. I was dressed appropriately. I felt strong and confident, my resume was flawless and I walked with a purpose. Each step screamed "I am coming for my job." It was that attitude that allowed me to land a job the same day. I was hired as a phone surveyor working for a communications company that conducted health surveys. The job description fit the criteria stipulated in the conditions of work release. The task of employment had been accomplished. That night I thanked God and Dress for Success. The next task would be to find suitable housing that would meet the approval of my Parole Officer. This would enable me to leave Phoenix House at the end of my six month stay. Many women were forced to go to Bay View Correctional facility in Manhattan because they were unable to secure an approved residence. Some made it and others continued to suffer in active addiction. I realized there was no one in New York that I could live with, without putting my recovery at risk. So I began networking on my job making co-workers aware of my situation. I wasn't ashamed and this enabled me to tell the truth of my struggle. I was amazed at how willing people were to help me. Sure enough God placed a woman by the name of Aretha in my path. We sat next to each other daily at work. After explaining my situation to her, she told me

Poetic Recovery

how her mother came to be imprisoned in the Bedford Hills Correctional Facility where she died. Aretha told me she understood how it felt to not be able to come home to your loved ones as result of waiting for her own mother who never returned. What she did next, touched my heart. She offered me a room in her home, in the Bronx. She told me she would charge me a rent I could afford. She made it so cheap I was able to save enough money to move out on my own. Aretha was another angel who played a major role in my recovery process. My housing was approved by my parole officer on July 17th 2001. My room had been prepared for me to move in. Aretha had two beautiful children and worked very hard to keep them fed, clothed and housed. She inconvenienced herself in order to help me. She is another blessing that was strategically placed in my life to cushion my journey through recovery. We always talked at work; however, living together gave us a lot more time to get to know each other. Because we worked the same shift we rode the subway together nightly. This was a good thing because 170th Street and Jerome Avenue was an unsavory part of the Bronx. At night prostitutes, addicts, and drug dealers colored every street corner, stoop and hallway. We used our commute time to learn about each other's lives and future goals. It was during one of these conversations I discovered Aretha was once a substance abuse counselor. She explained to me that the work schedule of a residential counselor did not allow her any quality time with her children who were at an age when her presence in their lives was greatly needed. I explained to her that I was interested in going into the field of substance abuse. It was then that she gave me the information I would need to attend a school in the Bronx known as Act I. That night I made a conscious decision to do what I believed would impact the lives of so many men and women who were struggling with the disease of addiction. I called the school the next day, and completed a phone screening to ascertain whether or not I was appropriate for the training. Sure enough I was given a date to come in, test, and interview. I was confident I had passed the written test, after which I was told I would be contacted as to whether or not I would be brought back for a second interview. In addition to my willingness to do whatever it took to break into the field of substance abuse, I knew I would require computer skills. Having witnessed the counselors of Phoenix House struggle to complete assessments and psycho socials on the computer I knew it would be beneficial to learn how to navigate the computer. It was clear the more skills I had the more marketable I would become.

Poetic Recovery

Chapter Fifty Five

I located and enrolled into a free computer class I could attend before I went to work in the afternoons. Global Institute was located on 125th street. My guidance counselor Ms. Edna worked closely with me to ensure I was assigned the classes that would best assist me in my upcoming role as a substance abuse counselor. I studied hard and caught on fast. I placed daily phone calls to Act I, inquiring as to whether or not I was selected to return for a second interview. It was five months before I received an invitation for the second interview. Time whizzed by and I began to navigate the computer effortlessly. I went to school, work and came home until I found an N.A. (narcotics anonymous) meeting near Aretha's house. This was perfect because I was told it was crucial to my recovery process that I make ninety meetings in ninety days. It wasn't enough just to attend the meetings, I had to introduce myself and say "I am an addict." More importantly I had to get a sponsor and some phone numbers to call in the event I had the urge to smoke crack. I was told that I would be working the steps once I acquired a sponsor. I had never attended an N.A. meeting in the free world though I was familiar with the format from the volunteers who came to the prisons and Phoenix House. These volunteers are known as H & I (hospitals and institutions). The meeting I attended was called 7 am in the Bronx. I attended my meetings daily and met some very wonderful people with whom I shared my story. I found a sponsor who asked me to tell my story to the group which I did without hesitation. The most important person at any meeting is the newcomer. I made my presence known and asked questions. I preferred the 7 am meetings because, I was accustomed to getting up at 5 am (still on prison schedule).To this day I still wake up at 5 o'clock every morning. It ensures that I am not late for any appointments, and gives me plenty of time to prepare myself properly. This meeting gave me that extra source of support I needed to begin living life on life's terms in the free world. The day finally came when I received the phone call from Act I. When I did, I fell to my knees and thanked God. The interview was held in a large conference room at a huge round table. Each of the instructors was present during the interview. A barrage of questions was thrown at me and I responded intelligently and without hesitation being careful to include the question in my response. The final question was, would I be willing to wait another six months in order to begin my training. My answer was emphatically yes!

  During the next six-months I continued my classes with the Global Institute polishing up my computer skills and learning different soft-ware programs. Knowing that all client information was now being entered into

Poetic Recovery

computers I began practicing how to write progress notes and treatment plans thanks to Aretha. My busy schedule was subject to the approval by my Parole Officer after all I was the property of New York State. This also meant that no decision of mine was final. I made my initial visit to my Parole Officer, and found her to be a fair woman. I explained to her what I was doing and what I wanted to do. She said that she was genuinely shocked, I still had a job and more importantly that I had filled every free moment with an activity that would assist me in becoming a productive and responsible member of society. Ms. Burchen permitted me to have a life while on Parole. She explained to me she would never be responsible for violating me and sending me back to prison. She explained she was giving me my life back. All I had to do to keep it was, stay clean and under no circumstances have any police contact. My weekly visits soon became bi-weekly and soon thereafter monthly. Needless to say I never violated, in any shape form or fashion. I submitted to random urinalysis testing. The ongoing joke was that my urine is so clean you could drink it. The New York State Division of Parole is as tough as a Parolee makes it. I learned that change is not suppose to be a comfortable transition, it is suppose to ultimately become a learning experience that teaches you a lesson, unless of course you are a sucker for self-inflicted torture. I for one am not! I was

Life Don't Rhyme

anxious to learn about whether or not I had been accepted into Act One. I was now calling them 2-3 times a week in hopes of being given an official start date. I was notified in the mail that I had been accepted and was given a start date. I reflected on the last time I waited for what I wanted and I received it. It was one thing to believe that true change had taken hold of my life; it was another, to see it. It was during my active addiction that I taught my family members how to treat me, having stolen and lied to every single member. I have accepted the fact that forgiveness will come in time. This also meant I could not demand that anyone forgive me. After all, I was the one at fault. I knew forgiveness would come when I could show and prove. Not in my time, in thine. I learned I would have to teach everyone I had harmed during my active addiction how to treat me all over again. My family was very accommodating. No one would drink alcohol when I was around. My brothers assisted me in any way they could as long as it ensured that their big sister was clean and sober. Darien and Brandon were living where my mother once lived in The Lionel Hampton houses on St. Nicholas Ave. They had separate apartments with their wives and children. My mother took on the task of early Saturday morning phone calls. Though it was only to chat, it was her way of making sure I knew she was proud of me and my efforts in recovery. I explained to her the importance of surrounding

Poetic Recovery

myself with other people in recovery, so as not to subject myself to negativity in any form. She laughed during this conversation, telling me if I am tempted to do wrong, just think about the consequences. She went on to tell me that my healthy decision making would become second nature. She was right as always.

    Next course of business was to check on my best friends Doretta, Arian and T. I stopped by to see Doretta and her mother, Mina. They were still living in the same apartment in the St. Nicholas Housing Project. Throughout the years Doretta and her mother had become my mainstays; without them I would not have survived the streets that held me hostage for 29 years. I could always count on them for the truth, a good meal, something to wear and a place to lay my head during my active addiction. Doretta was still doing her thing, but it did not include smoking crack. She had cleaned up her act. However, our friend Arian was going through her own voluntary madness of using illicit drugs and alcohol. It was Arian's better than attitude and impaired breathing that kept her from smoking crack cocaine. However, she still exhibited the behaviors of a crack head and was in need of help. I was asked by my girlfriends Doretta and T where we could send Arian to get some help. I gave them the same information that assisted me in jump starting my life. I knew she wasn't about to listen to me, because I had stolen from her to get high, so it was up to Doretta and T to convince Arian to seek help. Like all addicts Arian was in denial about the severity of her disease of addiction. I knew I was not going to be the one she would listen to and knowing this I left it in the hands of my higher power. Like all families of addicts, Arians family was greatly impacted by her drug use. Because we all are friends we each had a personal stake in making sure we did all we could to get Arian into treatment. Her decision to go was greatly influenced by Doretta and T. Arian took the suggestions and completed treatment and is now living happy, joyous and free. Now that's what friends are for!

    Next I took time to locate Earnest and found he was still in recovery living clean and sober. We saw each other from time to time and went out on dates, sober meetings, the movies, shopping, dinner and concerts. We were getting to know each other sober and that was quite a challenge. The one thing I admired about Earnest was that he had kept his word to himself and had not returned to smoking crack or using any other form of drugs including alcohol. I learned there is no such thing as a healthy relationship between two people who engage in the insanity of drug use. We spent so many of our earlier years together destroying our lives and now we were blessed to enjoy the blessings of recovery together. He remains one of my dearest friends, and source of support.

Poetic Recovery

Chapter Fifty Six

The fact remained that I was still an addict who needed to remind herself daily about the negative behaviors that often lead to relapse mode. Though I was not active, I had some negative behaviors that if I permitted myself to rationalize right and wrong would taint my recovery process. I encountered many situations that required immediate healthy decision making. Had it not been for internalizing the tools taught to me by Mr. Major, I could have easily put my recovery and my freedom at risk.

I continued to report to my Parole Officer and submit to random urine testing as required. I was informed that I was scheduled go to the Parole Board on September 11, 2001. I was up early as usual and very excited. At 9:00 in the morning I was sitting on the edge of the bed watching and listening to the news; when a news broadcast flashed across the screen reporting that one of the Twin Towers had been hit by an airplane. My first thought was that I was watching a movie. I called Earnest and he said that he was watching the same show. He went on to tell me it was an actual event in progress. It just didn't register, and I continued to prepare to leave for the Parole Board. When I arrived at Bayview where the Parole Board was meeting I saw large billows of black smoke coming from the direction of the World Trade Center and thousands of people walking across the

Life Don't Rhyme

Westside highway in droves. I was informed that my Parole hearing had been cancelled and that I would be notified when it would be rescheduled. The next thing I did was try to contact Earnest, and my family members. My Brother Brandon's wife worked in Tower One. I called him first and was relieved to hear the voice of my sister n law on the other end of the phone. I asked her what made her stay home from work, and she told me she needed to clear the children's rooms of old toys. I then asked to speak to my brother Brandon she answered quickly informing me that he was at work on the road stuck in traffic. I then called my brother Darien and he and his wife and children were all safe at home. My last call was to my sister Allana who was also home with her children. Next I called my other siblings who were all out of state and found them to be safe. I thanked God for being in charge.

The weight of fear had been lifted from my heart and I was able to call my mother and report to her that all of her children were safe. My oldest brother Kenan contacted her, letting her know that he too was safe in Rochester, New York. I was still walking around in downtown Manhattan in shock. I walked around for hours trying to gather information about the attack on the World Trade Center. When I finally reached Harlem where my brothers and sister lived we all gathered in Brandon's home. We called our mother to report that we were all together and that she could put her worries to rest. We prayed

Poetic Recovery

together and thanked the Lord for being spared. We prayed for the souls who had perished civilians, firemen and police officers. Because I worked in communications, I was unable to work due to major phone lines being destroyed.
I received assistance from the Red Cross and my church, Brotherhood Baptist Church of Brooklyn. Pastor Mungin and his family along with my church family made sure I was able to pay my rent. Aretha was not pressing me for any money because we were in the same boat and worked together. I learned that human compassion has no limits in the face of adversity. I didn't meet with the Parole Board until November, and my Parole was granted! I was commended for having maintained two jobs in addition to going to school. I moved out of Aretha's home after having received my income tax return. I found a room near Aretha's home and my fellowship group. I felt a need to surround myself with positive people doing positive things. I rented a large room, in a two family home and shared the kitchen and bathroom with another female who was in recovery. I maintained my same routine of attending my 7am meetings afterwhich I went to my computer class, and then work. I was saving my money to move into a real apartment, because I wasn't comfortable sharing a bathroom and kitchen. I had enough of sharing in prison. It was May 2002 when I received the call informing me that I had been accepted into Act I

counseling school. I was to begin classes the following Monday. They made me aware that random urine testing would be conducted and that anyone with positive results would be immediately terminated. I knew then I was on my way to becoming a counselor. My personal writing slowed due to my hectic schedule and massive amounts of homework. I had moments when I needed to write my feelings down on paper so that they wouldn't get away from me. I didn't shirk on my responsibilities to myself and becoming a better person. I knew that recovery required one hundred percent and that was what I vowed to give. Six weeks before actual classes were to begin I and my peers were required to work in a nursery with plants. I was devastated, that I had to come in contact with dirt (soil). I went up in my head alone and rationalized that if I came to school professionally dressed I would be put in an office position. That was not the case. I was told in no uncertain terms that if I did not comply I would be terminated. I'm an addict and I had to try something. I immediately weighed my options and went home only to return in jeans and sneakers. I carried a change of clothes daily my image was dictating my actions and that was a problem. I was later informed that this project was put in place to teach us what plants and clients have in common. It became a very therapeutic learning experience. In Act I we were often confronted by staff as to why we wanted to pursue the field of

Poetic Recovery

counseling. When I was posed with this question I responded "because I know having survived my own drug addiction that I am capable of teaching and encouraging others to believe that there is life after active addiction."
I learned that my thinking would be constantly challenged by this team of instructors and I rose to the occasion each and every time. I found this practice to be advantageous; because I knew first hand that our clients would be challenging us daily. My school hours forced me to drop one of my jobs. My computer class brought me up to speed and I was able to complete assignments with ease. I lived and breathed counseling just as I did my recovery. I studied hard and recieved good grades. The atmosphere was one I was familiar with. Aside from the clinical information Act I took on the guise of a therapeutic community. It was treatment on a smaller scale. I was comfortable in a treatment setting having come through the CASAT program with Mr. Major and Phoenix House. Earnest and I became reacquainted with each other, and he respected the journey that I was a part of. Though we were great friends, to resume a relationship would mean that requirements would have to be met. I had come to know enough about myself to know that before I committed myself to a relationship with someone else I had to establish a healthy relationship with myself. That meant I was not going to settle for anything but the best. I was not going to put anything that would

Life Don't Rhyme

improve me on the back burner because it wasn't conducive to someone else's life. I was not going to take shortcuts to get to where I wanted to be in my career. I was going the long route so I wouldn't miss anything. Instant gratification is a major character defect among addicts in recovery. It was told to me that addicts want what they want when they want it and adults get what they get when they get it.

Because I have incorporated this slogan into my life, my standards have scaled new heights. Ernest was equipped with climbing equipment and became my biggest fan. He rooted for me in every area of my life. I found comfort in knowing that whatever I wanted to achieve he was there to cheer me on. We began a courtship and a new friendship flourished. The good thing is, we both know each other's faults and shortcomings. It is good to live with someone who knows when you are full of it. They can stop you before you go overboard. This is the role Earnest plays in my life. I call his bluff and he calls mine.

Poetic Recovery

REQUIREMENTS

LOVE ME BECAUSE YOU WANT TO

LIKE ME BECAUSE YOU CAN

LAUGH WITH ME, BECAUSE I'M FUNNY

NEED ME BECAUSE YOU HAVE MY SUPPORT

SHARE WITH ME BECAUSE I HAVE SO MUCH TO GIVE

EMBRACE ME BECAUSE I WILL EMBRACE YOU

CRY WITH ME AND WE CAN DRY EACH OTHERS TEARS

DO THESE THINGS AND MORE

AND OUR LOVE WILL SOAR

THESE ARE MY REQUIREMENTS FOR ANY RELATIONSHIP

NO THEY DON'T COME ALL AT ONCE

EACH ONE TAKES TIME

BUT TIME IS SHORT AND SHOULD NOT BE WASTED

UNDERSTAND WHAT TRUE COMMITMENT IS AND MEANS

BEFORE YOU TASTE IT

Life Don't Rhyme

Chapter Fifty Seven

Earnest and I established some ground rules that would make sure we didn't waver in any aspect of our recovery. No alcohol or drugs. We kept it simple! Earnest liked to keep it simple he knew firsthand how easily it was for me to complicate things. I found comfort in knowing that our future would never again be threatened by the use of illicit drugs or alcohol. We would often attend a movie in the same area where we once consumed narcotics. Lenox Avenue looked so very harmless at first glance. Her streets still adorned the decor of drug use and sales. This day I was meeting Earnest, we were going to the movies. Coming out of the subway at 116th street and Lenox Avenue my eyes scanned the ground. This was an old habit I acquired during my active addiction. My eyes zeroed in on empty crack vials and bags that littered the street. I immediately caught myself and regained my focus. I continued to walk uptown to 118th Street where Earnest was waiting at Maurice's Laundromat. When his eyes met mine he could see the anxiety in my face. He recognized what I was feeling and instantly took hold of my hand and said "let's go." I could see the neighborhood had undergone some radical changes. As for my disease of addiction it was still on its job. What the disease didn't know was that I too, had a job, to live! Some of the same people we once surrounded ourselves with

Poetic Recovery

were still living in their same addictive madness. Many were still using crack. Others had gone to prison, or died. Very few had awakened from the nightmare of addiction. Now that I am awake I take delight in knowing that I survived that chapter of my life. I have no need for a wakeup because I welcome going to sleep at night in my own bed in my own home.

Life Don't Rhyme

TO BE

TO BE OR NOT TO BE HIGH

THAT IS THE QUESTION

WHETHER IT IS NOBLER TO FACE LIFE SOBER AND FREE

OR GO IN AND OUT OF JAILS TO WHICH I HAVE NO KEYS

LIVING LIFE ON LIFE'S TERMS
THIS METHOD OF LIVING I MUST LEARN

RUNNING FROM REALITY
CAN SOON BECOME A FATALITY

ADDICTION CAN ONLY TAKE YOU FROM
THE BEAUTIFUL PERSON YOU COULD BECOME

SO WHEN ANSWERING THE QUESTION
SHOULD I GET HIGH?

KNOW IF YOU RESPOND WITH THE WORD YES
YOU HAVE TRULY FAILED YOURSELF

NOT ALLOWING YOURSELF TO LIVE
YOUR LIFE TO THE FULLEST

UNDERSTAND IF YOU ANSWER NO

YOU WILL BE ABLE TO SHOW YOURSELF AND THE WORLD

A PERSON YOU ARE NOW PROUD TO KNOW

Poetic Recovery

Chapter Fifty Eight

Throughout my addiction, there were three people who continued to allow me into their lives. They remain my friends, and have never once passed judgment on me; Billy from the Pimp's Palace, Doretta, and Lonnie Jenkins from the Big Track.
No matter what shape I was in these three people continued to take care of me.
They didn't hesitate to tell me how badly I was fucking up. They always offered me a place to sleep, food to eat, and a lecture accompanied with a harsh dose of the truth. For their love and support I will always be grateful. The words of these three people made an impact on my mind and in my life. I always left them entertaining the thought that I could change, without putting forth any effort. Hearing the truth about me from others never penetrated my crack riddled mind unless it came from those three people. I deeply cared what they thought of me. It amazes me that I had enough brain cells left to devote to my counselor training program. Of course I realize that this blessing was through no power I possessed. I was able pass my exams and receive an internship and a job before anyone in my class (cycle 11). Recovery continues to show me the many blessings I was told would come my way as long as I didn't use drugs. As a result of my continued involvement with Dress for Success and the Professional

Life Don't Rhyme

Women's Group, I have appeared on The Iyanla Vanzant Show, Life and Styles, CNN and The Today Show on NBC. The purpose of these appearances was to inform women of the dynamic work done by Dress For Success. All of its efforts are geared toward guiding women who have survived adversity toward self sufficiency. As a recipient of the services provided by Dress for Success it has been my personal responsibility to inform everyone I meet about my journey through addiction and more importantly, my journey through recovery. All women are my sisters, and all women need the support of one another. Dress for Success is nothing short of an army of angels. Their troops are equipped with professional attire, knowledge, and an international network that spans the globe. My relationship with this organization is one of love and respect. It is important for women who face adversity to know and believe that there is life after a storm. My passion lies with those people I service daily. Though it is a job, it has also become a personal obligation. Having devoted 29 years of my life to the use of drugs, I am eternally grateful to all the people who encouraged and motivated me to return to the land of the living. They are my heroes.
I define my life as a work in progress. More importantly I do not regret any portion of my life, because it has created the person I have become. I have learned that where there is God there is Success.

Poetic Recovery

The author currently resides in Bronx New York. She works as an alcohol and substance abuse assessment specialist for an agency in Manhattan. She continues to work toward helping to save the lives of those who continue to suffer from the horrors of addiction. She is available for comments, motivational seminars and workshops.

Visit her at zoesheppard.biz or zsheppa@aol.com